The History
of the
AMERICAN PRESIDENCY

The History
of the
AMERICAN
PRESIDENCY

JOHN BOWMAN

JG
PRESS

Published by World Publications Group, Inc.
455 Somerset Avenue
North Dighton, MA 02764
www.wrldpub.net

ISBN 1-57215-420-9

Printed and bound in China by SNP Leefung Printers Limited.

Page 1: *The White House in Washington DC circa 1886. The presidential residence looks much today as it did then.*

Page 2: *The presidential inauguration takes place outside the Capitol building in Washington DC. This photograph shows Ronald Reagan's first inauguration, in January 1981.*

Page 4: *The bald eagle is the symbol of the United States of America. It is shown here in classic form atop a red, white and blue shield clutching an olive branch (for peace) and arrows (for war).*

CONTENTS

INTRODUCTION

In the years since 1789, when George Washington took the oath as the first president of the United States, 41 men have held the office. Some have been more successful in this position than others – such presidential giants as Abraham Lincoln and Theodore Roosevelt have become legendary figures in American history and seem to embody the very essence of America, while the names of Millard Fillmore and Benjamin Harrison have drifted into obscurity. Between these extremes lies a whole range of careers of varying achievement. And the portrait gallery of America's presidents exemplifies the history of the country in the sheer diversity of their origins and upbringings,

Right: *This well-known statue of Abraham Lincoln is in the Lincoln Memorial in Washington, DC.*

Opposite: *The White House in Washington, DC, has been the home of every president since John Adams.*

Below: *The Jefferson Memorial in Washington, DC, uses elements of Thomas Jefferson's own design for the Rotunda at the University of Virginia. A full-length statue of Jefferson, the third president of the United States, is inside the memorial building.*

their experiences and careers, and their geographical, political, social, material and intellectual differences.

Many US presidents have been lawyers – but no one would say that Lincoln's life or Franklin D Roosevelt's, is summed up, let alone linked to the others', primarily by this professional thread. There have been a number of soldiers, some professional military men, and even a few generals – Ulysses S Grant and Dwight D Eisenhower, as well as Zachary Taylor and William Henry Harrison. A number of career politicians, men who were bred for their country's service and who spent most of their lives in elective office, have served as president; but what a spectrum is covered by such men as John Quincy Adams, who returned to the House of Representatives after his term as president, William Howard Taft, who retired as Chief Justice of the Supreme Court and Lyndon B Johnson, once Speaker of the House –

or for that matter, by Harry S Truman and John F Kennedy, both of whom were senators. And how would one categorize men like Woodrow Wilson, once a professor of history, the multi-faceted Thomas Jefferson, Herbert Hoover, a mining engineer, Theodore Roosevelt, who wrote 28 books or Ronald Reagan, an ambitious actor.

None is typical in one sense, but all, taken as a whole, reflect American history and some of the many people who have settled in the United States. Thus looking through the illustrations of their lives and administrations provides a sense of looking at the nation's family album. The pictures comprising this book illuminate those diverse aspects of their lives that made them Americans as well as presidents. And that, in the end, is what makes a pictorial history both entertaining and enlightening: The great and influential men of our past and present are here connected to our daily lives and our heritage.

George
WASHINGTON
1732-1799

As the first president of the new United States of America, George Washington assumed a tremendous responsibility, both in the immediate sense of pressing obligations and in the long-term sense of historical judgment. Most fair-minded and realistic students of history would agree that Washington succeeded on both levels. Yet to look at his background there was little to suggest in his upbringing and education that this man was going to be a remarkable leader.

The son of a prosperous planter, trader, and iron foundary operator, George Washington was born in Westmoreland County, Virginia, on 22 February 1732 and spent his youth in the usual pursuits of the country gentry: riding, hunting, fishing and boating. His formal schooling ended when he was 15, and although he was obviously intelligent and literate – during much of his life he kept careful diaries and expense accounts – he was not the student of history and ideas that contemporaries such as Jefferson and Madison were. If anything inspired young George it was his half-brother Lawrence's tales of military service. Washington wanted to join the Royal Navy, but his widowed mother refused to let him go to sea, and he settled for the profession of surveyor. Between the ages of 15 and 21 Washington spent much of his time in the wilderness on surveying expeditions.

In 1753 Washington became a major in the Virginia militia which served with the British regular forces during the French and Indian war in the western reaches

Left: *George Washington, Commander in Chief of the Colonial Army, receiving the salute of the field at the Battle of Trenton, 1777. Washington became the first president of the United States in 1789.*

Top right: *Engraving depicting the young Washington on one of his surveying expeditions.*

Right: *The south front of Mount Vernon, Washington's home.*

Overleaf: Washington Crossing the Delaware, *by Emanuel Gottlieb Leutze.*

of the colonies. It was a most trying period, physically and in other respects, for Washington actually experienced far more defeats than victories, losing many of his men in engagements and surrendering Fort Necessity to the French.

When the fighting stopped, Washington returned to Virginia to assume the role of country gentleman at Mount Vernon (although he did not legally inherit it till 1761). He married a wealthy widow, Martha Dandridge Custis, who had two young children; became active in church and social affairs; and above all managed his property – farmlands, buildings and slaves. He served in the Virginia House of Burgesses from 1758 on, but he introduced no major legislation and made few speeches. Although he had written privately of his dislike for the 'despotism' of the British, this was perhaps more the natural resentment of a prosperous property owner than a call to the barricades. Washington did attend the First Continental Congress in September 1774, where he impressed his fellow delegates with his military knowledge and sound judgment, but he made no speeches and was not appointed to any committees. When, at the Second Continental Congress in June 1775, Washington was named Commander in Chief of the Colonial Army,

By His EXCELLENCY

GEORGE WASHINGTON, Esquire,

GENERAL and COMMANDER in CHIEF of the Forces of the UNITED STATES OF AMERICA.

BY Virtue of the Power and Direction to Me especially given, I hereby enjoin and require all Persons residing within seventy Miles of my Head Quarters to thresh one Half of their Grain by the 1st Day of February, and the other Half by the 1st Day of March next ensuing, on Pain, in Case of Failure of having all that shall remain in Sheaves after the Period above mentioned, seized by the Commissaries and Quarter-Masters of the Army, and paid for as Straw

GIVEN under my Hand, at Head Quarters, near the Valley Forge, in Philadelphia County, this 20th Day of December, 1777.

G. WASHINGTON.

By His Excellency's Command,
ROBERT H. HARRISON, Sec'y.

LANCASTER: Printed by JOHN DUNLAP

it was over the objection of some New Englanders and in part to placate the Southerners.

During the Revolution itself, to be sure, Washington emerged as both a strong leader and the symbolic embodiment of the colonists' aspirations. But neither Washington nor most of his fellow leaders offered the colonists a very clear idea of what the new nation would actually be like; they were simply fighting to be free of British rule. Meanwhile, thousands of Loyalists openly rejected the Revolution, while a number of rebellious officers resented Washington's position, to the point of attempting a coup. Although Washington did inspire great loyalty by his presence and example, as at Valley Forge, many soldiers deserted or quit as soon as their terms of enlistment were up. He seldom had more than 10,000 troops under his command at any one moment, and these were spread dangerously thin. But Washington and his commanders and troops won the engagements that counted, in part with the aid of the French. When the Revolution finally ended at Yorktown, he was universally regarded as a hero. When he resigned his command he told his officers, 'I have grown gray in your service and now find myself growing blind.' He then retired to Mount Vernon to devote himself to improving his own property and developing various public works projects.

In 1787 Washington was summoned to the Constitutional Convention as the head of Virginia's delegation, where his fellow delegates elected him president of the convention. As such, he presided over the fiercely partisan proceedings, making sure the delegates remained in Philadelphia to finish the job. By the time of the first presidential election, George Washington was the virtually unanimous choice of the electorate (although it should be said that only a minority of adults had the vote).

When Washington assumed the presidency on 30 April 1789, he was well aware of his unique situation: 'I walk untrodden ground,' he wrote. His first four years, in fact, were largely occupied with the most fundamental organization of the new government – creating machinery for administering oaths of office, setting taxes on imports, establishing a system of federal courts, providing for the finances of the government, founding a

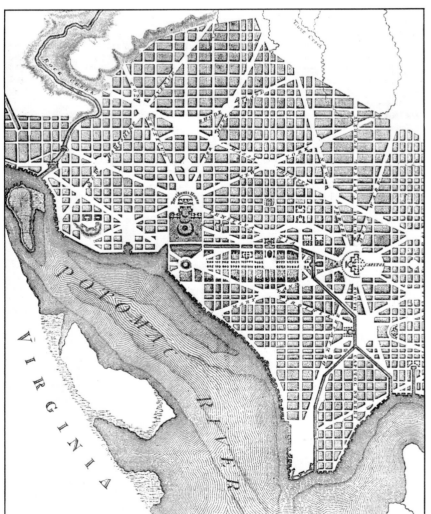

Above: *George Washington taking the oath as first president of the United States, 30 April 1789.*

Left: *The planning of the federal capital was supervised by George Washington in 1791. Washington DC became the nation's capital in 1800.*

Opposite, top: *Washington and Lafayette at Valley Forge during the infamous winter of 1777-8.*

Opposite, below: *During the hard winter at Valley Forge, Washington required residents of the area to contribute grain to feed his hungry troops.*

national mint, planning for a new capital, and much else. Washington did his best to remain above the details and turmoil. He believed in letting his department heads act independently and tried to avoid interfering in the legislative and judicial branches. Washington's 'Olympian' approach, however, was not the way of most of his contemporaries; political parties inevitably began to form, centering primarily around either the position represented by Hamilton and his Federalist colleagues – calling for a strong central government – or the position represented by Jefferson and his supporters – calling for more states' rights.

Washington was ready to retire after his first term but was persuaded by men such as Madison and Jefferson that the new nation might founder without him to lead it. The American voters seem to have agreed, for he won a second term unanimously. His second term, however, proved considerably more stormy than the first, particularly as the result of his attempts to remain neutral in the ongoing conflict between Britain and France. The crisis centered on the signing of the treaty that John Jay had negotiated with Britain. Although it had dealt effectively with matters of trade and the British forts on the frontier, it had done nothing to prevent the British from stopping American ships at sea and pressing their seamen. Washington's signing of this treaty brought him probably the most hostile criticism of his long career of public service. Another difficult decision was forced upon him when farmers in western Pennsylvania rebelled against paying federal taxes on homemade whiskey. In 1794, Washington was obliged to send 15,000 federal troops to put down this potential rebellion.

As his second term drew near its end, Washington made no secret of being tired of the presidency, particularly of the increasing rough-and-tumble of political parties. He resurrected the farewell address that he and Madison had written four years previously and published it in Philadelphia's *American Daily Advertiser* (on 19 September 1796), and in the spring of 1797 he retired to Mount Vernon to take up once again the active management of his extensive properties. In 1798 he was commissioned Lieutenant General and Commander in Chief of the American forces 'raised or to be raised' in a threatened conflict with France, but the threat dissolved and Washington returned to Mount Vernon. His last letter, to Alexander Hamilton, mentioned the need for a national military academy, a reminder that Washington had always been a soldier. Shortly thereafter he took a long horseback ride on a cold, snowy day; became ill (probably a streptococcal infection); and died on 14 December 1799.

Washington's passing was mourned throughout the United States and Europe – in France, Napoleon called for 10 days of mourning. In the years that followed, the United States could hardly find enough ways to honor him. Hardly a city or town does not have a Washington Street or Avenue. Many geographical features are named after him. He is the only American to have a state named after him, as well as the nation's capital. His portrait is on both the one dollar bill and the twenty-five cent coin and on many of the postage stamps printed in the United States since 1847. In the 1920s, when debunking of historical idols was in fashion, some critics made much of Washington's limitations – his aloof manner, his distaste for the more democratic elements of political life, his commitment to preserving the prerogatives of the propertied class. But no one has ever fully succeeded in removing Washington from his pedestal of international esteem. To be called 'the George Washington of his country' is an accolade that most statesmen today would be happy to accept.

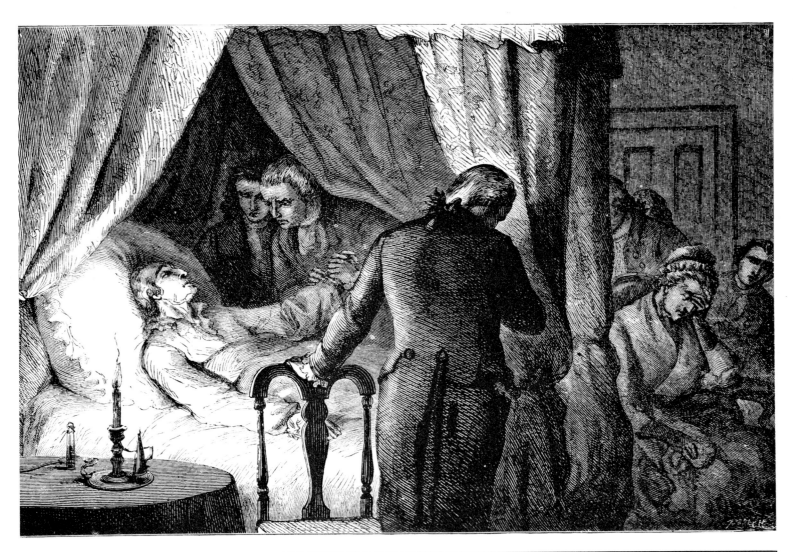

Above left: *The Whiskey Rebellion, 1794. Pennsylvania distillers resented the first federal tax, which was on spirits. Tax collectors were sometimes tarred and feathered, as shown here.*

Above: *Washington retired from the presidency in 1797 and died at Mount Vernon on 14 December 1799.*

Right: *Washington's obituary, from the* New York Gazette and General Advertiser: *'. . . in every quarter of the Globe, where a free Government is ranked amongst the choicest blessings of Providence . . . The Name of Washington will be held in veneration.'*

Previous pages: *Washington the country gentleman, shown fox-hunting in this painting by John Ward Dunsmore.*

New-York, December 21.

Columbia Mourns!

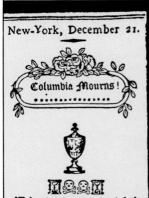

IT is with the deepest grief that we announce to the public the death of our *most distinguished* fellow-citizen *Lieut. General George Washington.* He died at Mount Vernon on Saturday evening, the 13th inst. of an inflammatory affection of the throat, which put a period to his existence in 23 hours.

The grief which we suffer on this truly mournful occasion, would be in some degree aleviated, if we possessed abilities to do justice to the merits of this *illustrious benefactor of mankind*; but, conscious of our inferiority, we shrink from the sublimity of the subject. To the impartial and eloquent historian, therefore, we consign the high and grateful office of exhibiting the life of *George Washington* to the present age, and to generations yet unborn, as a perfect model of all that is *virtuous, noble, great*, and *dignified* in man. Our feelings, however, will not permit us to forbear observing, that the very disinterested and important services rendered by *George Washington* to these United States, both in the Field and in the Cabinet, have erected in the hearts of his countrymen, monuments of sincere and unbounded gratitude, which the mouldering hand of Time cannot deface; and that in every quarter of the Globe, where a free Government is ranked amongst the choicest blessings of Providence, and *virtue, morality, religion*, and *patriotism* are respected, THE NAME of WASHINGTON WILL BE HELD IN *veneration.*

And as along the stream of TIME, his name
Expanded flies, and gathers all its fame,
Oh! may our little bark attendant sail,
Pursue the triumph, and partake the gale!
While Statesmen, Heroes, Kings, in dust repose,
Whose *sons* shall blush their *fathers* were his foes.

CONGRESS, Dec. 18.

Immediately after reading the journal, General Marshall came into the House of Representatives, apparently much agitated, and ad-

dressed the Speaker in the following words:
Information, sir, has just been received, that our illustrious fellow-citizen, the Commander in Chief of the American army, and the late President of the United States, is no more!

Though this distressing intelligence is not certain, there is too much reason to believe its truth.

After receiving information of a national calamity so heavy and so afflicting, the House of Representatives can be but ill fitted for public business. I move you therefore, that we adjourn.

The House immediately adjourned.

The Senate also adjourned in consequence of this distressing intelligence.

Extract of a letter from a gentleman of veracity, dated Alexandria, Dec. 10, 1799.

" General Washington died last night, under the adjunct attention of Doctors Crock and Dick, of Alexandria, and Doctor Brown, of Port Tobacco, Maryland."

A gentleman last evening politely favored us with the following extract of a letter from Alexandria, dated December 15.

" I mention to you the truly melancholy event of the death of our much beloved general GEORGE WASHINGTON—He made his exit last night between the hours of 11 and 12 after a short but painful illness of 23 hours. The disorder of which he died is by some called the Crupe, by others an Inflamatory Quinzy, a disorder lately so mortal among children in this place, and I believe not until this year known to attack persons at the age of maturity.

My information I have from doctor Dick, who was called in at a late hour. Alexandria is making arrangements to show its high esteem for him. We are all to close our houses, and act as we should do if one of our family had departed. The bells are to toll daily until he is buried, which will not be until Wednesday or Thursday. He died perfectly in his senses, and from doctor Dick's account perfectly resigned. He informed them he had no fear of death, and that his affairs were in good order that he had made his will, and that his public business was but two days behind hand."

☞ *See the Resolutions of the Common Council.*

17

John
ADAMS
1735-1826

John Adams was something of a paradox. His great brilliance and knowledge made him one of the indispensable forces in the creation of the United States. His quirky temperament made him a quarrelsome politician and an ineffective president. Born in Braintree (now Quincy), Massachusetts, on 31 October 1735, Adams graduated from Harvard and was admitted to the bar in 1758; his extensive knowledge of British law and history was to serve him well in his later writings. Influenced by the radical ideas of his cousin Sam Adams, John entered politics in 1765 by pamphleteering against the Stamp Act. Five years later, surprisingly, he defended the British soldiers involved in the Boston Massacre, but that was merely a statement of principle – he was already on the rebellious side and was soon to be a leader at both sessions of the Continental Congress. In 1776 the colonies' critical break with England came when, in Congress, Richard Henry Lee made the motion in favor of independence. John Adams seconded that motion. He also helped Thomas Jefferson edit the Declaration of Independence, which he shepherded through its debate and adoption in Congress.

Left: *John Adams became second president of the United States in 1796.*

Above: *The Boston Tea Party, 16 December 1773. Adams was of strongly colonial sympathies and supported such acts as the rebellion against the tea duty.*

Below: *Adams was born at 133-141 Adams Street in Braintree (now Quincy) Mass, in 1735. This painting from 1849 shows John Adams' house on the right, and his son John Quincy Adams' house on the left.*

Opposite: *The White House in Washington DC during Adams' final term as president.*

Above: *Abigail Adams at the age of 22, the wife of John Adams. They were the first residents of the White House.*

Below: *A cartoon of 1797 showing anti-French feeling following the XYZ Affair, in which France demanded bribes to renew diplomatic relations with the United States. An undeclared war resulted.*

His writings continued through the Revolution, laying groundwork for the government to come. Adams wrote most of the influential Massachusetts constitution of 1780, then served for seven years as a diplomat to France, Holland and Britain. Along with Benjamin Franklin and John Jay he negotiated the 1783 Treaty of Paris that ended the Revolution and cemented independence. Thereafter, concerned about the weaknesses of the Confederation, Adams wrote articles on constitutional issues that were influential to the deliberations of the Constitutional Convention. Adams was elected George Washington's vice-president in 1789. In his usual crusty style, he wrote of that office 'My country has in its wisdom contrived for me the most insignificant office that ever the invention of man contrived or his imagination conceived.'

It was clear all along that Adams was Washington's heir apparent, and he was duly elected president in 1796. According to the procedure of that time, the candidate with the second highest number of votes became vice-president. For Adams, that man was Thomas Jefferson, whose intractable States' Rights convictions were to make him a foe of Adams from within

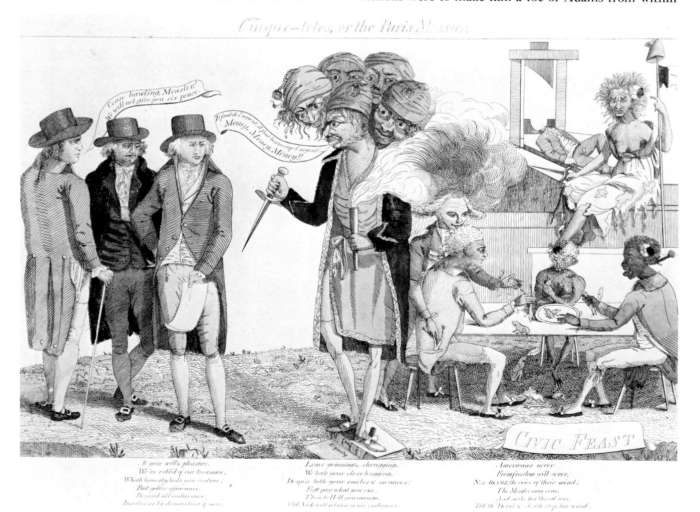

the administration (a good example of why the procedure for electing the vice-president was eventually changed).

At the outset of his administration, Adams tried to maintain a nonpartisan stance between the Federalists and the Jeffersonian Republicans. The primary problem of his administration was troubles on the high seas with Britain and France, as both these warring countries were seizing American merchant sailors and vessels. With the Federalists lusting for outright war, Adams worked doggedly for peace while building up the armed forces. In 1797 Adams sent three secret peace commissioners, dubbed X, Y and Z, to France, which demanded of them large bribes for agreeing to a treaty. Adams publicly released these details, and America began an undeclared naval war with France. As controversy grew on both sides of the Atlantic, Federalists drew up the Alien and Sedition Acts, which virtually banned criticism of the government. Adams signed the acts, in effect a blow against democracy itself.

Indeed, Adams' ideas about democracy were, at best, unmodern. While recognizing the role of the people in electing representatives, he also believed that government itself should be the responsibility of an intelligent elite whose actions should be subject to minimal popular restraints. In this he went counter to the Jeffersonian and democratic temper of the times. In addition, he ignored the developing two-party system (which had not been foreseen in the Constitution). The final blow to his administration came when Adams managed to reach an agreement with France that forestalled war. It was a diplomatic masterstroke, but it also enraged Alexander Hamilton and the Federalists. Adams had thus managed to antagonize both parties, while the country at large seethed with resentment over the repressive Alien and Sedition Acts by which the administration sought to mute public criticism. (Among those arrested for violating the acts was Benjamin Franklin's grandson, a newspaperman).

Despite public relief at Adams' avoiding war, Jefferson won the election in 1800. Before he left office Adams hastily made a number of judiciary appointments, including naming the anti-Jefferson John Marshall as Supreme Court Justice. Adams then retired to 25 years of political inactivity at his home in Braintree. During those years he engaged in voluminous correspondence, most notably with his old nemesis Jefferson, with whom he finally was reconciled. Adams' spirit of competition never dimmed: as he died on 4 July 1826, exactly 50 years after the signing of the Declaration of Independence, he murmured, 'Thomas Jefferson still lives.' Adams was wrong; Jefferson had expired a few hours before.

Thomas
JEFFERSON
1743-1826

America was indeed lucky in its founding fathers. Among the greatest of these was Thomas Jefferson, who helped create the nation with his Declaration of Independence and for 50 years thereafter was one of the most brilliant thinkers and leaders the new country possessed. He was, among other things, a farmer, lawyer, family man, diplomat, architect, linguist, scientist, philosopher, inventor, amateur musician, founder of a university and president of the United States. Perhaps it was the last role that he least enjoyed, though he occupied the presidency with the same breadth of mind and commitment to service that he demonstrated in all his public life.

Left: The third president of the United States, Thomas Jefferson, had a distinguished background as an eloquent advocate of the natural rights of man.

Top: The signing of the Declaration of Independence, 4 July 1776, as seen in this painting by J Trumbull. Jefferson was responsible for the drafting of this influential document.

Descended from a well-known planting family of Albemarle County, Virginia, Jefferson was born on 13 April 1743. He attended the College of William and Mary, and his first career was that of a lawyer. In 1769, already anti-British, he entered the Virginia House of Burgesses, where he wrote an important patriotic pamphlet, *A Summary View of the Rights of British America*. There one already finds his ideas of the natural rights of men, which were inspired by the philosophers of the European Enlightenment.

In 1775 Jefferson was dispatched to the Continental Congress, where he soon became a leading member. His lucid eloquence on paper brought him the assignment of writing the Declaration of Independence, which he made into one of the great documents of history, a statement of human liberty and governmental responsibilities that has influenced democratic thought ever since.

Jefferson spent the Revolution as governor of Virginia. During that period he wrote into law the landmark Bill for Establishing Religious Freedom and began the process of ending the African slave trade in Virginia. (Jefferson was one of many early American

Left: *Monticello, the home of Thomas Jefferson.*

Above: *Alexander Hamilton, a Federalist, was often at odds with Jefferson.*

Right: *The signing of the US Constitution, 1787.*

Below: *Jefferson departing for his inauguration, 1801.*

statesmen who both deplored slavery and owned slaves. He made some anguished and all-too-accurate prophecies of the bloodshed slavery would cause.) From 1781–83 Jefferson lived at his beloved estate of Monticello, beginning work on a major study of the natural history of Virginia.

After serving again in the Continental Congress, Jefferson succeeded Franklin as minister to France, reporting home the developments of the French Revolution, whose triumphs and horrors influenced him deeply. He returned to find the United States Constitution completed. At first he was not happy about its concentration of power, but he was placated on learning of the impending Bill of Rights. Named secretary of state in Washington's first cabinet, Jefferson found himself in an increasingly adversarial position to treasury secretary Alexander Hamilton. The split was classic and inevitable: Hamilton and the Federalists were urban, aristocratic, business-oriented and pro-British; Jefferson saw the country as a nation of thinking farmers, distrusted commerce and wealth and was pro-French. By about 1893 the Jefferson faction had become the first opposition party in America. Then called the Republi-

cans, they became the Democrats a few years later. Neither Jefferson nor anyone else at the time foresaw a fully developed two-party system, but he nonetheless helped bring it about.

Running a close second to John Adams in the 1796 election, Jefferson became, by the procedure of the time, vice-president. He spent four years working more against Adams than for him. Especially galling to Jefferson and the Republicans were Adams' repressive Alien and Sedition Acts. Jefferson and his ally James Madison sponsored resolutions that promulgated the idea of state nullification of unconstitutional laws. This concept, in theory a blow for civil liberties and human rights, was in the end to contribute its part to the slow buildup of the Civil War.

In 1800, with the Federalists in disarray, Jefferson easily unseated John Adams from the presidency, though he only narrowly defeated the third candidate, Aaron Burr, in an election that had finally to be decided in the House. Jefferson moved quickly to placate Federalists in Congress. His success set a valuable precedent for the peaceful transfer of power from one party to another. Believing in a restrained central

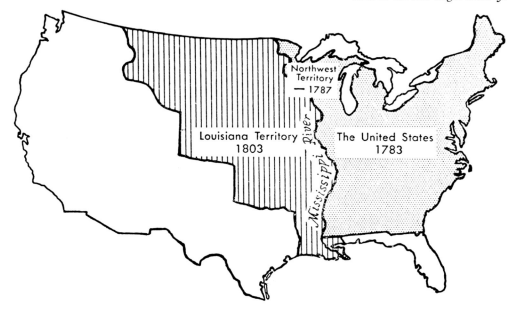

action, Jefferson exceeded his own ideas of presidential power, but he knew a bargain when he saw one. This departure from strict constitutional interpretation more than doubled the land area of the country. Wishing to know more about the continent, Jefferson then sent Lewis and Clark on their historic expedition to the Pacific.

Jefferson was easily re-elected to a second term in 1804, but already seeds of dissension had been sown. Despite his considerable popularity, Jefferson had been the victim of vicious personal attacks. His religious beliefs in particular were liberal enough to have him branded 'antichrist' by some New England Congregationalists. His vice-president, Aaron Burr, had resigned and in 1806 was arrested on charges of conspiracy. Jefferson was uncharacteristically vindictive toward Burr. His efforts to influence Chief Justice John Marshall during Burr's trial only deepened the rift between himself and Marshall after Burr was acquitted.

Far more vexing were the effects of the war between France and Britain, both of whom were preying on American shipping, with Britain stealing American sailors on the high seas. Jefferson, believing in a weak

government and executive branch, Jefferson worked with Congress indirectly, persuading rather than decreeing. His first term was generally triumphant.

In 1801 Jefferson initiated the new nation's first major military operation by sending a naval squadron to put down the Barbary Pirates in Tripoli. Two years later came the masterstroke of his presidency. He had sent ministers to Napoleon to try and buy New Orleans from France. Instead, they found themselves being offered the whole Louisiana territory. With Jefferson's blessing, the ministers made haste to cement the deal before Napoleon changed his mind. By taking that

Top: *The official proclamation of the Louisiana Purchase, 1803.*

Above: *The Louisiana Purchase doubled the area of the United States.*

Previous pages: *This painting by DM Carter shows Stephen Decatur boarding a Barbary pirate gunboat during the Tripolitan War.*

presidency, was in a quandary. Either he had to go to war, which he resisted, or to exceed his powers once again. He chose the latter, imposing an embargo on all foreign exports in an effort to put economic pressure on the belligerents. The results were disastrous. His action had no effect on England or France, but it devastated the American economy. With Jefferson's popularity at its nadir and the nation near rebellion, Congress repealed the controversial embargo at the end of his presidency.

Leaving office in 1809, Jefferson returned to Virginia. The country soon forgave his embargo, admiring him as the 'Sage of Monticello.' His last great task was a labor of love, the founding of the University of Virginia. He designed its extraordinary campus, ushering in the Classic Revival in America. Becoming reconciled with Adams, Jefferson began a long and historic series of letters with his old friend. The two men died on the same day: 4 July 1826, the 50th anniversary of the signing of the Declaration of Independence. Along with Benjamin Franklin, Jefferson would be remembered as the American closest to the ideal of the Renaissance man, and as a shining champion of human liberty.

Left: *Lewis and Clark on the Columbia, by Harold von Schmidt. They explored the far Northwest to the mouth of the Columbia River, 1804-06.*

Top: *An English cartoon on the Embargo Act, showing Napoleon prompting Jefferson. The unpopular embargo was later repealed.*

James
MADISON
1751-1836

One of the most celebrated 'fathers of the American Constitution,' James Madison would, during his presidency, be called upon to lead his country through the most traumatic events it had experienced since the Revolution.

Madison was born to a wealthy planting family of Port Conway, Virginia, on 16 March 1751 and was graduated from the College of New Jersey (now Princeton) in 1771. There he had read numerous works by liberal European Enlightenment philosophers that deeply influenced his thinking on politics and society. Five years after graduation, the young Madison helped draft the Virginia constitution. He was elected to the Continental Congress in 1780. In his four years there his ideas concerning government took shape, his central concept being that of the 'separation of powers,' a system of checks and balances among the three branches of government. This principle was finally to pervade every part of the Constitution.

Returning to Virginia, Madison became a member

Left: *An advocate of the 'separation of powers' at the Continental Congress of the 1780s, James Madison became president of the United States in 1808 and held office for two terms.*

Above: *USS* Constitution *and HMS* Java *in action, December 1812, by C R Patterson.*

Right: *Perry's victory on Lake Erie, 10 September 1813. Print by Currier and Ives.*

Left: In Mud To His Ears –
*a War of 1812 cartoon showing
George III between a Kentucky
rifleman and a Louisiana
creole.*

Below left: *The British forces
captured and burned
Washington DC in 1814.*

Top right: *Original copy of
'The Star Spangled Banner.'*

Below right: *On seeing Old
Glory still flying over
Baltimore's Fort McHenry on
14 September 1814, Francis
Scott Key was inspired to write
'The Star Spangled Banner,'
which later became the
national anthem.*

of the House of Delegates, securing passage of Thomas
Jefferson's landmark religious freedom bill. Unsatisfied
with the weak Articles of Confederation, Madison campaigned for a new United States Constitution. In the
Constitutional Convention of 1787 Madison's ideas and
brilliance in debate contributed mightily to the adoption
of the epochal document. Subsequently, with Alexander
Hamilton and John Jay, Madison contributed to *The
Federalist*, a classic commentary supporting ratification
of the new Constitution. Madison was elected to the
House of Representatives in the new government,
crowning his labors by sponsoring the Bill of Rights.

Though he was close to Washington, Madison in
the 1790s found himself closer in thinking to Thomas
Jefferson. They both took the lead in opposing the
policies of Hamilton and the Federalists, which they
felt gave too much power to the central government and
too much favor to the wealthy. More or less uninten-
tionally, their faction became the first opposition party –

first called the Republicans, later the Democrats. In
1797 Madison left Congress. Working in Virginia
against President Adams' Alien and Sedition Acts, he
wrote a resolution which said that states had the right to
reject federal laws. Thus, Madison unwittingly helped
open the Pandora's box of nullification, one day to
become the proximate cause of the Civil War.

When Jefferson became president in 1801, Madison
became his secretary of state and close partner for eight
years. Despite Jefferson's problems as president, the
Republican party itself remained strong and took
Madison to the presidency in 1808. Madison now in-
herited the main difficulty that had frustrated both him
and Jefferson before: the drain on American shipping
caused by the depredations of France and, especially,
Britain, which had been hijacking American seamen for
years. In 1812, and without particular enthusiasm,
Madison gave in to the inevitable and declared war on
Britain. He found himself in the same dilemma that

The Star-spangled banner.

O say! can you see by the dawn's early light
What, so proudly we hail'd at the twilight's last gleaming
Whose broad stripes and bright stars, through the clouds of the fight
O'er the ramparts we watch'd were so gallantly streaming
And the rocket's red glare — the bomb bursting in air
Gave proof through the night that our flag was still there?
O say, does that star-spangled banner yet wave
O'er the land of the free & the home of the brave? —

Jefferson and all similarly inclined presidents faced. Believing in a mild and restrained central government and no standing army, how was he now to take strong and decisive action in a military emergency? Madison was no better able to solve this quandary than was Jefferson.

The result was a muddled war effort. Adams appointed ill-qualified war secretaries, and the disorganized troops given the defense of Washington allowed the British to burn the capital in the summer of 1814. (American legend remembers Dolley Madison fleeing from the burning White House with Stuart's portrait of Washington in hand.) Except for a series of naval victories, the war consisted mostly of American humiliations. In 1814 the British decided to stop fighting, but the Treaty of Ghent at the end of the year gained little of consequence for the United States (though it did return the status quo).

Just before the treaty took effect, however, Andrew Jackson won a victory over the British in New Orleans, and in the general rejoicing the nation decided it had at last proven its mettle. Madison spent his last two years in office enjoying great popularity, using his new strength to charter the Second Bank of the United States and fix some protective tariffs (neither of which were at all Jeffersonian). Dolley Madison meanwhile ensured her reputation as the most brilliant hostess the capital had seen. Leaving office much acclaimed, and with his chosen heir, James Monroe, newly elected, Madison retired in 1817 to a career as elder statesman in Virginia. He died in Orange County on 28 June 1836.

James
MONROE
1758-1831

Though he was not the thinker and philosopher that his mentors, Jefferson and Madison, were, James Monroe was arguably the better leader in action. Monroe was born to a planter's family in Westmoreland County, Virginia, on 28 April 1758. After two years of study at the College of William and Mary he joined the Continental Army during the Revolution, where he saw much action, was wounded in the Battle of Trenton and spent the terrible winter of 1777 at Valley Forge. Returning to Virginia in 1780, Monroe began to study law with Thomas Jefferson, who became his life-long friend.

Inspired by Jefferson, Monroe plunged into politics and over the next 25 years engaged in an extraordinary array of endeavors. Elected to the Virginia House of Delegates, he moved on to the Confederation Congress in 1783. His reservations about the concentration of power in the national government made him initially

Left: *James Monroe, fifth president of the United States.*

Top right: *Osceola, leader of the Seminole Indians of Florida during their war with the United States in 1818.*

Above: *General Washington and his men at Valley Forge during the War of Independence. Monroe was very active during the war and was wounded during the Battle of Trenton.*

oppose Virginia's ratification of the United States Constitution. But finally he took a seat in the United States Senate in 1791, where he joined with Jefferson and Madison in forming the Republican party. After serving as minister to France under President Washington, Monroe became governor of Virginia in 1799.

In 1803 President Jefferson sent Monroe and Robert Livingston to France as envoys. They were supposed to convince Napoleon, who had just gained Louisiana from Spain, to concede navigation rights on the lower Mississippi. Instead, they found themselves being offered the whole territory, and on Jefferson's approval snapped up the offer before Napoleon changed his mind. Soon after, Monroe was named minister to England, but when Jefferson rejected a treaty Monroe had negotiated with Britain, relations between the two cooled for some years.

Again elected governor of Virginia in 1811, Monroe resigned to become secretary of state for his old friend James Madison. On his return to Washington he was reconciled with Thomas Jefferson and settled into his job as the War of 1812 broke out. In 1814 he became secretary of war as well, replacing an inept occupant who

had very nearly lost the war. Soon peace came, and during the wave of prosperity that followed, Monroe was elected president in 1816, having been the heir apparent to Madison.

Monroe was a big, raw-boned, plain-looking and plain-speaking man. His great assets were a tact, honesty and charm that enabled him to work well with friends and rivals alike. Though a Republican, he made it clear that he was not going to be a partisan president. He worked especially hard to conciliate the Federalists, and they responded in kind (like most politicians of the time, Monroe was not at all reconciled to a two-party system). Owing to his efforts to smooth animosities, his first term came to be called the 'Era of Good Feelings'.

Much of a president's job in that era had to do with gaining and protecting territory and managing relations with countries having claims to adjacent territories. In 1818, a crisis arose when General Andrew Jackson pursued some hostile Indians into Spanish Florida. Amid the ensuing tumult, Monroe apologized to Spain, but soon thereafter Spain ceded Florida to the United States and Monroe peacefully gained a substantial amount of territory. Also resolved was a dispute over fishing rights in Newfoundland and Labrador.

and, to the amicable Relations existing between the United States and those powers, to declare that we should consider any attempts on their part to extend their system to any portion of this Hemisphere, as dangerous to our peace and safety. With the existing Colonies or dependencies of any European power, we have not interfered, and shall not interfere. But with the Governments who have declared their Independence, and maintained it, and whose Independence we have, on great consideration, and on just principles, acknowledged, we could not view any interposition for the purpose of oppressing them, or controlling in any other manner, their destiny, by any European power, in any other light, than as the manifestation of an unfriendly disposition towards the United States. In the war between those new Governments

Though Monroe accepted the rather un-Jeffersonian tariff and national bank that were already in place, he still believed, with Jefferson, in a mild and unassertive executive power. Thus he took no part in congressional debates on the Missouri Compromise of 1820, which banned slavery north of latitude 36 degrees 30 minutes. He supported the bill when it was passed but he was uneasy about its implications. Already sec-

tional tensions over slavery were beginning their long buildup toward the Civil War.

In the election of 1820 Monroe received all the electoral votes but one. Three years later he made his most historic initiative. Supported by his secretary of state, John Quincy Adams, Monroe rejected a British proposal to jointly discourage European intervention in Latin America. Instead, Monroe announced his own policy, which proclaimed American hostility to any outside colonization or interference in the Americas. Later known as the Monroe Doctrine, it closed the continent to further colonization.

Though his second term saw the return of partisan struggles, and his relations with Congress deteriorated, Monroe left office a much-loved figure, retiring to Virginia in 1825. He died at his daughter's home in New York City on 4 July 1831. Like his fellow pathbreakers, Adams and Jefferson, he died on the anniversary of the signing of the Declaration of Independence.

Left: *An election scene in front of the State House in Philadelphia in 1815.*

Below left: *Part of the Monroe Doctrine, in James Monroe's hand, from his message to Congress on 2 December 1823.*

Below: *The formulation of the Monroe Doctrine. Henry Clay is at the left and John Quincy Adams is seated next to him. James Monroe is standing. John C Calhoun is at the right of the door and Andrew Jackson is seated next to him.*

John Quincy
ADAMS
1767-1848

John Quincy Adams ascended to the presidency with more apparent qualifications than anyone before or since. He was a brilliant scholar and linguist whose political and diplomatic experience had begun at the age of 13; moreover, he had been deliberately groomed for the presidency by his father, John Adams. But in the end his tenure as chief executive proved only a brief and unsatisfactory episode in a lifetime of otherwise remarkable achievements.

Born in Braintree, Massachusetts, on 11 July 1767, by the time he was 14 Adams was secretary to the American minister to Russia and later traveled with his father on several diplomatic missions. He was graduated from Harvard in 1787, was admitted to the bar three years later, and, due to his active support of Washington's policies, was named minister to the Netherlands and then to Prussia. Elected to the United States Senate in 1803, he supported President Jefferson's policies, including the embargo. For that reason, angry Federalists forced his resignation from the Senate in 1808, a harbinger of difficulties to come. Over the next decade Adams was minister to Russia, chairman of the peace commission that ended the War of 1812, and minister to Britain. In 1817 President Monroe named Adams secretary of state, a post he filled very well indeed. Among his achievements were negotiating the acquisition of Florida and the Pacific Northwest from Spain (later called 'the greatest diplomatic victory . . . in the history of the United States') and writing major parts of the Monroe Doctrine.

It was only natural that Adams should climax such a remarkable record by winning the presidency, which he did in 1824. His troubles began even before he took office. He had gained fewer popular votes than his adversary Andrew Jackson, and the election was sent into the House. There Henry Clay switched his support to Adams, giving him the election. When Adams then named Clay secretary of state, the Jacksonians took up the cry of 'bargain and corruption' that would hound Adams throughout his term and split the Democratic-Republican party into two factions that were soon to become the anti-Jackson Whigs and the Jacksonian Democrats.

Adams had grand plans for the country but was unable to marshal the personal or party loyalty to realize them. In his diary he accurately described himself as 'cold, austere and forbidding.' His programs for strengthening the central government, controlling public lands and improving national transportation routes ran afoul of States' Rights interests; and his vice-president, John C Calhoun, the apostle of slavery and States' Rights, was sharply at odds with Adams' distinctly antislavery stance. Adams was equally unsuccessful in his efforts to make the country a self-sufficient power and a predominant influence in the hemisphere.

Jackson took the presidency from Adams in 1828. Two years later Adams began his long and distinguished tenure in the House, where he fought against slavery until his death on 23 February 1848 of a stroke suffered on the floor of the House. His descendants would carry on his family's tradition of scholarship and service into the twentieth century.

Left: *The Erie Canal, linking New York City with the Great Lakes, was completed in 1825. This and other improvements in national transportation routes encouraged commercial growth in the country and was one of President Adams' achievements.*

Right: *John Quincy Adams, sixth president of the United States, was elected by the House of Representatives when no candidate gained a majority of the electoral college.*

Andrew
JACKSON
1767-1845

Andrew Jackson was powerful and charismatic both as a military leader and as president. But as much as anything else, he was a symbol, representing to the common people a kind of populist ideal: the self-made country man fighting his way to highest office, his ability coming not from education but from integrity and moral courage. The first man outside the aristocratic Virginia dynasty to be elected president, Jackson more or less fitted that image, though among his qualities was a goodly measure of simple ambition and ruthlessness.

Jackson was born to an Irish immigrant family in the Waxhaw settlement of South Carolina on 15 March

1767. He received little formal schooling. After fighting in the Revolutionary Army, he studied enough law to be admitted to the bar, and in 1788 he moved to Nashville, Tennessee, to begin practice. In 1791 he married Rachel Robards, who unknowingly was still married to another man – the divorce she had presumed in effect came through only after her marriage to Jackson. The couple hastily arranged a new ceremony, but the damage was done: they were followed for the rest of their lives by rumors of impropriety, and Jackson regularly fought duels over the matter, on at least one occasion killing his opponent.

Jackson prospered enough on land speculation and other business interests to buy an estate near Nashville, called The Hermitage, in 1795. The following year he took part in the state constitutional convention and was elected to the United States House of Representatives. Moving to the Senate in 1797, he was forced by financial problems to return to Tennessee, where he became a

Left: *'Old Hickory,' Andrew Jackson, was the seventh president of the United States.*

Below: *Jackson as a boy refuses to clean the boots of a British officer during the War of Independence.*

Left: *One of a pair of English-made dueling pistols owned by Jackson.*

Right: *The Jackson ticket relied on support from the masses and advocated universal white male suffrage.*

Supreme Court judge. For some years he sat happily on the bench, where he was respected not so much as a learned judge but as an intuitively astute and fair one. In 1804, he began a long retirement to The Hermitage, and the public heard little of him until the outbreak of the War of 1812.

Having gained a commission as a major general, in 1813, already known admiringly to his troops as 'Old Hickory,' he led a successful expedition against the Creek Indians, who were allies of the British. Subduing the Creeks in the battle of Horseshoe Bend in 1814, he then captured Pensacola, Florida, and marched for New Orleans. There, on 8 January 1815, Jackson turned back a British assault with such a storm of rifle and cannon fire that the British suffered 2000 casualties to Jackson's 16. Immediately Old Hickory was celebrated as a hero around the country.

In 1818 Jackson came close to disaster when he chased some hostile Indians into Spanish Florida. Secretary of State John Quincy Adams managed to turn the ensuing crisis into a victory when Spain ceded

Above: *During the War of 1812, General Andrew Jackson battled the Creek Indians who were British allies. This engraving shows Jackson at the Battle of Tallushatchee, 3 November 1813.*

Right: *Jackson's victory at the Battle of New Orleans in the War of 1812 made him a national hero.*

JACKSON TICKET.

AMERICAN SYSTEM.

Speed the plough, the Loom & the Mattock

FOR THE ASSEMBLY
JOHN V. L. McMAHON,
GEORGE H. STEUART.

Florida to the United States. His reputation secure, Jackson was elected again to the Senate in 1823, but he soon set his sights on the presidency and mounted a strong campaign in 1824. The election turned out to be a historic showdown: Jackson received the most electoral votes but lacked a popular majority; the election was at last decided in the House when Henry Clay swung his vote to John Quincy Adams. When Adams then appointed Clay secretary of state, Jackson had his issue for the next election. 'Bargain and corruption,' he said, and the nationwide coalition he formed over the next four years took up the cry.

The campaign of 1828 was largely a mudslinging contest, with the camps of Jackson and John Quincy Adams vying to produce the most outrageous accusations. But 'bargain and corruption' or not, Adams had

manifestly been a failure as president. When the electoral votes were counted, Jackson had 178 to Adams' 83. From all over the country the working people who were beginning to think of themselves as Jacksonian Democrats flocked to the Inauguration, leaving the White House a tobacco-juice-stained shambles in their wake.

Jackson assembled around himself a group of cronies who came to be known as the 'kitchen cabinet.' With their help, he rewarded his followers with all the government jobs he could find, thus setting a pernicious and ineradicable precedent for patronage in American politics.

He soon came into conflict with vice-president John C Calhoun of South Carolina, who encouraged his state to nullify some high tariffs that Jackson defended. Southerner though he was, Jackson was a fervent Unionist and opposed to any hint of nullification. As tensions mounted Calhoun resigned. Fortunately, in 1833 Henry Clay created a compromise tariff that placated South Carolina, and once again the Union was calm for a while.

There are several curious aspects of Jackson's administration. A Jeffersonian by his own lights, he nonetheless was the inspiration for the party remaking itself in his rather un-Jeffersonian image: the modern Democratic party looks at Jackson as its founder. Yet

Top: Jackson's 'self-made man' image made his 1828 inauguration a wild celebration for the working people who attended.

Above: On 30 January 1835 Jackson defended himself against an assassination attempt and emerged unscathed.

Right: Jackson refused to become involved in Texas' bid for independence. This painting by Robert Onderdonk shows the Battle of the Alamo, in which the 187 defending Texans were massacred by a force of 3000 Mexicans.

Jackson was not essentially a party man, considering himself a representative of all the people – except perhaps the moneyed aristocracy, whom he hated. Finally, though by the force of his personality he in effect created the modern strong presidency, he nonetheless was a firm advocate of States' Rights.

It was for this last reason that Jackson opposed the United States Bank, campaigning against it in his re-election (over Henry Clay) in 1832. Much of his second term was spent fighting the rechartering of the bank, and by 1836 he had put enough of its funds into state banks so that rechartering failed. It was a victory for him, but the aftermath bequeathed a financial panic to Jackson's chosen successor, Martin Van Buren. Another

question of the era had to do with Texas' struggle for independence; Jackson stayed out of the way, refusing to annex the territory, which would inevitably have provoked domestic battles over the slavery issue. Though Jackson was proslavery, he was wise enough to try to keep the issue politically dormant.

Upon leaving the presidency in 1837, Jackson retired to The Hermitage at the peak of his popularity. He remained an active elder statesman until his death there on 8 June 1845. He had created a new era in American political life. The aristocratic style of the founding fathers was rarely to be seen again in the presidency, and the country took one more step toward a true democracy with opportunity for all.

Martin Van
BUREN
1782-1862

Though he only served one term and is among the less-remembered presidents, Martin Van Buren had rather more impact on the nation's political history than his reputation might imply. In fact, he both established one of the first powerful state political machines and was the man who solidified the two-party system. Van Buren was born in Kinderhook, New York, on 5 December 1782, the son of a farmer and tavern-keeper. He had no formal education beyond the age of 14, but by 1803 he had learned enough law to begin practice in Kinderhook. In 1814 he was elected as a Democratic Republican to the state senate, beginning a steady ascent in political life that took him to the United States Senate in 1821 and to the New York governorship in 1828. By then, using extensive patronage, he had formed his machine, called the Albany Regency, and had thrown its power behind his mentor, Andrew Jackson, the man who would shortly make patronage a nation-wide institution.

Perhaps Van Buren's most far-reaching effort during his first years in national politics was in fusing the factions of Jackson, Calhoun and William H Crawford into the political unit, the Democratic party, that brought Jackson to power in 1828. Van Buren adamantly maintained that a two-party system, hitherto regarded as an aberration, was actually the best way to approach democracy. American history has borne out that idea.

Van Buren was rewarded by becoming Jackson's secretary of state in 1829 and vice-president in Jackson's second term (replacing the disaffected John C Calhoun).

A master political operator and party man, Van Buren was always able to charm his way to victory – thus his nicknames 'the Little Magician' and, less complimentary, 'the Red Fox of Kinderhook.' His service to Jackson made him heir apparent, and he rode into the presidency in 1836 on Jackson's departing coattails.

Van Buren arrived in office facing a severe economic crisis: the depression of 1837, during which 618 banks failed. Too cautious to take bold action, Van Buren nonetheless worked throughout his term to establish what became the Independent Treasury Act of 1840, a measure that took federal funds out of state banks and gave the government exclusive control over its money. As tensions over slavery rocked Congress and the entire country, Van Buren trod a delicate middle path, deploring slavery while tolerating its continuation in the South. He astutely defused boundary disputes along the Canadian border, leading to the 1842 treaty that finally settled the boundary.

Van Buren's political downfall came with his unpopular war against the Seminoles in Florida and, especially, with his refusal to annex Texas (on the grounds that this would spread slavery and risk war with Mexico). Renominated by his party in 1840, he was soundly defeated by William Henry Harrison. Later presidential bids also failed. Van Buren finally retired to Kinderhook, where he died on 24 July 1862. Long before the Civil War he had made an ominous prophecy: 'The end of slavery will come – amid terrible convulsions, I fear, but it will come.'

Left: *Martin Van Buren was elected eighth president of the United States in 1837. His term was overshadowed by financial panic.*

Right: *Slaves on the 'Underground Railroad' being smuggled north to freedom. Though Van Buren refused to offer the 'slightest opposition' to slavery, he predicted it would eventually end 'amid terrible convulsions.'*

William Henry
HARRISON
1773-1841

Had he not occupied the office of president for one month before his death, William Henry Harrison would likely have earned only a footnote or two in history as a military man. Born in 1773 to an aristocratic and political family in Berkeley, Virginia, Harrison was well educated before taking up a military career. After several years of fighting the Indians, he was appointed the first governor of Indiana Territory in 1801. Over the next 12 years he proved himself a master of extracting land from Indians by whatever means necessary.

After some tribes had conceded, under duress, about two and a half million acres on the upper Wabash River, Shawnee leader Tecumseh and his brother, 'The Prophet,' formed a confederacy against white encroachment. Harrison led his forces against these Indians at the Tippecanoe River in November 1811. Despite the inconclusive nature of the battle, it gained him a national

reputation. In the War of 1812 Harrison became a brigadier general of Northwest forces, defeating the British and their Indian allies at the Battle of the Thames in Ontario. In that battle, one of the more important in the war, Tecumseh was killed.

Harrison astutely used his military reputation and popular anti-Indian views to win political office. He entered the United States House of Representatives in 1816, and in 1825 was elected to the Senate. After several years of retirement in Ohio, in 1836 he came to the attention of the Whigs, who saw in him a military hero popular enough to oppose the Jacksonian Democrats. Harrison lost to Van Buren in that election, but the Whigs immediately geared up for the next. The 1840 campaign was unlike any before: an out-and-out circus. The sophisticated Harrison and his running mate, Southern sympathizer John Tyler, were portrayed as just plain folks in the 'Log Cabin and Hard Cider' campaign. Whigs showered the country with campaign hats, floats, model log cabins and barrels of cider; they taught the nation to sing 'Tippecanoe and Tyler Too,' with its refrain of 'Van, Van is a used-up man.' It was the first genuine two-party campaign, and the first in which candidates traveled all over the country. Harrison made nearly two dozen speeches to crowds of more than 50,000 people. Image and exposure, not issues, reigned supreme.

The campaign worked handsomely, and Harrison trounced Van Buren. His inaugural address showed his lack of political experience when he promised to defer to the leaders of Congress. That address, made by an exhausted man in a cold rain, was his last major effort; from that exposure he contracted pneumonia and died on 4 April 1841. Yet his campaign had provided the model for many a campaign to come.

Left: *William Henry Harrison had been depicted as a 'log-cabin, hard-cider candidate.' He proved to be rather less than hardy; he died one month after his inauguration in 1841.*

Right: *The ninth president of the United States, William Henry Harrison. The candidate for the new Whig party, he was elected by an overwhelming majority thanks to Whig campaign tactics.*

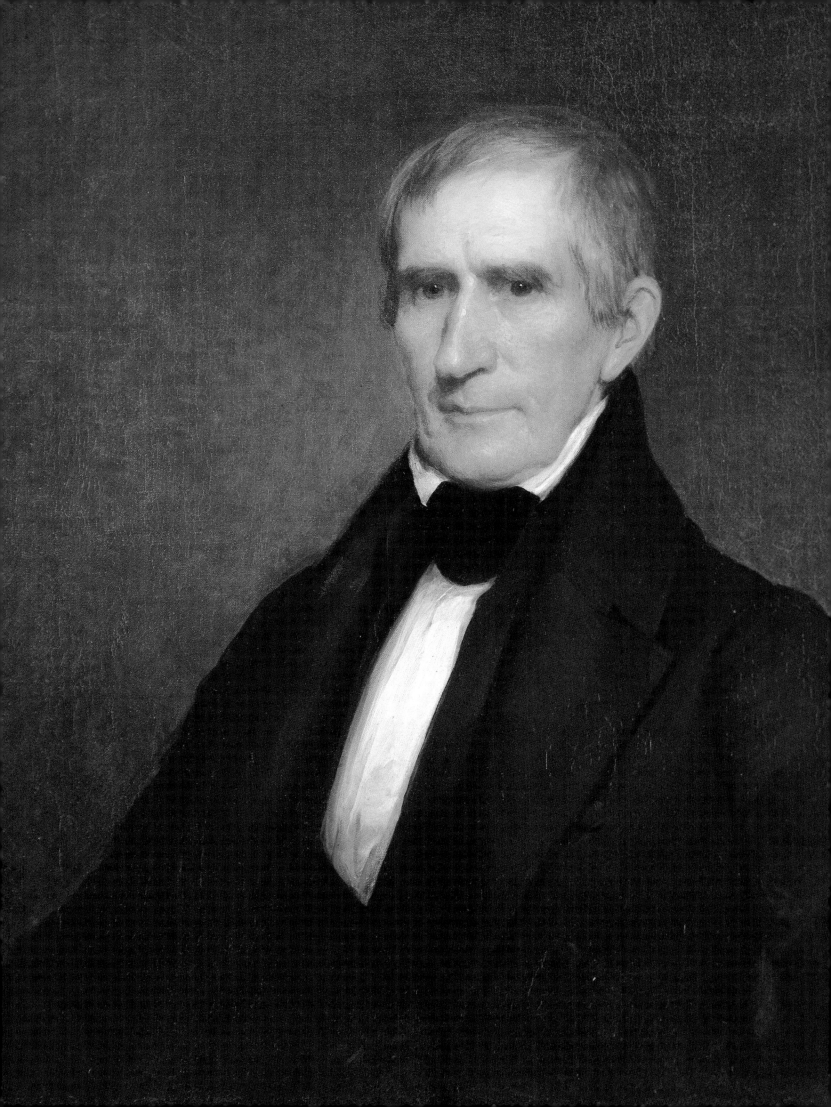

John
TYLER
1790-1862

The first man to ascend to the presidency on the death of the incumbent, John Tyler arrived in office with little public support. He had been placed on Harrison's ticket mainly to strengthen Southern votes, which had been wooed by his States' Rights stance. A man of consistent and inflexible principles, Tyler ended his career by casting his lot with the Confederacy at the outbreak of the Civil War.

Tyler was born to an aristocratic farming family in Greenway, Virginia, on 29 March 1790. After graduating from the College of William and Mary he was admitted to the bar in 1809 and elected to the state legislature two years later as a Jeffersonian Democratic Republican. He ascended steadily on the political ladder, and before he was 40, he was elected to the United States House of Representatives (1817), the governorship of Virginia (1825), and the United States Senate (1827). In those days, Andrew Jackson was the fulcrum around which American politics swung. Tyler was essentially anti-Jackson, but in the election of 1828 he supported Jackson over John Quincy Adams, whom he liked even less. Tyler made his name as a States' Rights man, which meant that he tolerated slavery, though he disagreed with it in principle. Accordingly, Tyler vigorously opposed the Missouri Compromise of 1820 on the grounds that Congress should not regulate slavery. His departure from the Senate was dramatic and characteristic: instructed to vote in favor of expunging a censure of Jackson from the record, he resigned rather than follow that order.

As an anti-Jacksonian, Tyler was taken up by the Whigs, and as such he was elected with Harrison in the 'Tippecanoe and Tyler Too' campaign of 1840. Upon Harrison's death, Tyler at 50 became the youngest president thus far. He proceeded to alienate his own party, vetoing two bank bills submitted by arch-Whig Henry Clay. In response, Clay convinced Tyler's entire cabinet to resign.

Despite being a president at odds with his own party and popularly derided as 'His Accidency,' Tyler did achieve some progress in his tenure – ending the Seminole War, reorganizing the Navy, reaching a trade agreement with China and encouraging pioneers to settle on unoccupied lands. Most notably, he annexed Texas at the end of his term, which Van Buren, fearing war with Mexico, had declined to do. Tyler ended his term with few supporters; some Democrats proposed to nominate him in 1844, but the idea was soon dropped in favor of Polk.

Tyler retired to his Virginia plantation, rising again to the public eye in 1861 when he organized and chaired a peace conference in Washington. The conference failed to forestall the Civil War. Thereafter Tyler endorsed secession and was elected to the Confederate Congress. Before taking his seat he died in Richmond, Virginia, on 18 January 1862.

Opposite: *John Tyler, tenth president of the United States.*

Top: *Tyler succeeded to the presidency upon the death of Harrison in 1841. Here he is shown getting word that President Harrison is dead.*

Left: Great Prize-Fight of the American Eagle Against the Wolf and the Alligator. *In this 1844 cartoon, Spain (alligator) and Britain (wolf in sheep's clothing) interfere in the US question of whether to admit new states to the union as slave states.*

James Knox
POLK
1795-1849

James K Polk was born in Mecklenburg County, North Carolina, on 2 November 1795. He grew up in Tennessee, was graduated from the University of North Carolina, and entered the Tennessee bar in 1820. Soon he was involved in politics as a Jacksonian Democrat, serving in the state legislature and then in Congress. In 1834–39 he was speaker of the House, leaving that position to become governor of Tennessee.

His ascension to the presidency was sudden and unexpected, following as it did two unsuccessful bids to be re-elected governor. Polk became the 1844 Democratic nominee on the ninth ballot and was the first major-party 'dark horse' candidate. (His opponent had been Van Buren, whose opposition to annexing Texas stalled his otherwise certain candidacy). Polk was chosen as an expansionist and took to that role vigorously, adopting the Democratic slogan 'Fifty-four forty or fight' (referring to the latitude claimed by Oregonians as their rightful boundry with Canada) and promising to 'reannex' Texas (which Tyler did just before leaving office). Narrowly winning the election over Whig Henry Clay, Polk made his position clear in his aggressive first message to Congress. The phrase 'manifest destiny' had recently been coined to signify American domination of the continent; Polk made it clear that he was determined to do his part to achieve it.

He made Mexico an offer of thirty million dollars for New Mexico and California. When Mexico refused, Polk sent General Zachary Taylor to provoke hostilities, which Taylor dutifully did, occupying land claimed by Mexico. The Mexicans started shooting on cue. Polk declared war forthwith and American forces made steady progress against the disorganized Mexican army. At the same time there was a considerable battle of opinion in America; the public wanted the land but were not so sure about taking it by force. Among the many protesters were Henry David Thoreau, who went to jail rather than pay war taxes, and Ralph Waldo Emerson, who prophesied, 'Mexico will poison us.' (He was thinking mainly of the inevitable slavery question which would follow the war.) Even some army officers, such as young Ulysses S Grant, deplored the war while they fought it.

For well or ill, the war was won. In the 1848 Treaty of Guadalupe Hidalgo, Mexico gave the United States over 500,000 square miles that included the future states of California, Nevada, Utah, most of New Mexico and Arizona and parts of Wyoming and Colorado. Texas joined the United States with its boundary on the Rio Grande. For all this territory the United States paid Mexico $18,250,000. Meanwhile, Polk had settled the Oregon question with Britain, fixing the boundary at 49 degrees without a fight. In addition to his territorial acquisitions, Polk re-established the independent treasury and reduced tariffs. However, he largely ignored the imminent struggle over whether the new territories were to be slave or free. More imaginative minds than his saw that this was the most crucial issue of all.

By 1848, Polk had methodically accomplished all but one of his promises, and he fulfilled the last one by refusing, as he had said he would, to run again. Exhausted by his extraordinary labors, Polk returned to Tennessee after Zachary Taylor's inauguration. He died three months later, on 15 June 1849.

Left: *Eleventh president of the United States, James Polk. A believer in 'manifest destiny,' he negotiated the Oregon boundary with Britain and re-annexed Texas.*

Right: *The Battle of Molino del Rey, 8 September 1847. Polk used force to gain a huge chunk of land from Mexico, and paid $18.25 million for it. The border was established at the Rio Grande.*

Zachary
TAYLOR
1784-1850

Like Jackson and Harrison, Zachary Taylor came to the presidency mainly on the strength of military glory; unlike them, he had never before been elected to office. Great general that he was, he tried manfully to master the political process, but before he could do so, death mastered him. Once again a vice-president of second-rate abilities had to take over. In a time of great peril to the Union, a time that more than ever called for bold and experienced leadership, America's luck seemed to falter.

Born in Orange County, Virginia, on 24 November 1784, Taylor joined the Army in 1808 and stayed in it for most of the next 40 years. He was a dutiful and courageous soldier who rose through the ranks, fighting in the War of 1812, the Black Hawk War and the Seminole wars. Thereafter, he commanded all troops in Florida and in the Army of Occupation on the Mexican border. By the time of the Mexican War he was already admired as 'Old Rough and Ready.'

In March 1846, President Polk ordered General Taylor to provoke Mexico into shooting first, and Taylor followed those orders by blockading a Mexican town. After the first skirmish, Taylor wired the president, 'hostilities may now be considered as commenced.' He went on to win battles at Palo Alto and Resaca de la Palma even before war was officially declared. Named a major general, he won more important victories at Monterey and Buena Vista. (In the latter engagement his army was outnumbered four to one by the forces of General Santa Anna.) By the end of the war, in 1848, Taylor's name was a household word across America, and thus he attracted the attention of the Whigs, who were ever on the lookout for a winning candidate.

Taylor had never even voted in a presidential election, but in the 1848 convention, the Whigs nominated him over Henry Clay and Daniel Webster. Taylor and running mate Millard Fillmore then went on to win over the Democrats, who were divided between Lewis

Cass and Martin Van Buren. The major question then facing the country was whether the vast territories gained in the Mexican War should enter the Union with or without slaves. Though born in the South and a slaveholder, Taylor had a Northern outlook: he believed that slavery could continue in the states that already had it, but that it should not be extended to new territories. The South saw in this both an attack on the institution of slavery and a potential invasion of States' Rights, and not for the first time, Southern leaders talked of secession. Meanwhile the Senate began working up to the Compromise of 1850 that would put off the final catastrophe for a decade. While these issues were coming to a head, Taylor achieved the one clear accomplishment of his administration: the Clayton-Bulwer Treaty with England establishing joint control of a projected canal across the isthmus of Central America. But Taylor was not to survive to see the resolution of any of the central issues that beset his presidency: he died suddenly in Washington on 9 July 1850 at the age of 66.

Left: *Twelfth president of the United States, Zachary Taylor.*

Top right: *Taylor served as general during the Mexican War. This engraving shows the Battle of Buena Vista, 1847.*

Overleaf: *This painting by William G Brown shows General Zachary Taylor and his staff after the Battle of Buena Vista. It was commissioned to help promote Taylor, known as 'Old Rough and Ready,' as the Whig presidential candidate.*

Millard
FILLMORE
1800-1874

Assuming the presidency on the untimely death of Zachary Taylor, Millard Fillmore proved a more genial figure than his predecessor, and one more willing to compromise. Unfortunately, the country was now so divided on the issue of slavery that there was all too little left to compromise about.

Fillmore was born in Cayuga County, New York, on 7 January 1800. He had virtually no education before the age of 18, but within five years of that age he had made himself a lawyer. Before long he was elected to the New York state assembly as a member of Thurlow Weed's anti-Masonic party. His major accomplishment there was to sponsor a bill ending imprisonment of debtors. Fillmore entered national politics in 1833 as an anti-Jackson member of the House, where he gravitated to the Whigs and became chairman of the Ways and Means Committee. In 1844 Fillmore ran unsuccessfully for governor of New York and then settled down to the job of state controller until the Whigs tapped him as Taylor's running mate in 1848.

When he became president, Fillmore broke with Weed and allied himself with Whig leaders Henry Clay and Daniel Webster, the latter becoming his secretary of state. The central issue of the time was a Whig bill designed to ease sectional tensions over slavery and thereby preserve the increasingly tenuous Union. Eventually called the Compromise of 1850, the bill, among other provisions, admitted California to the Union as a free state, allowed New Mexico and Utah to choose for themselves whether to allow slavery and restricted slavery in the District of Columbia. Most partisans grudgingly accepted these provisions, but a final provision enraged antislavery forces: the Fugitive Slave Act, which mandated the forced return of runaways from anywhere in the country. Fillmore signed the Compromise, and then made a point of enforcing its most divisive element, the Fugitive Slave Act. Though Fillmore's approach may have placated the South, it lost him the nomination in 1852 and greatly strengthened abolitionist sentiment in the North.

Fillmore had thus failed to achieve the nearly impossible major task all presidents faced in that era: reconciling North and South. One of the few triumphs of his administration occurred when he sent Commodore Matthew Perry to Japan, and, after some 150 years of isolation, Japan signed a treaty with the United States in 1854. Ignored by the Whigs in 1852, Fillmore ran for president with the Know-Nothing party in 1856 but received only eight electoral votes. He retired to an active life in the local affairs of Buffalo and died there on 8 March 1874. Essentially a good-hearted and even competent president, his qualities had nevertheless been insufficient to his times.

Below: *The landing of Commodore Perry at Yokohama, Japan, 8 March 1854. Soon afterward the Japanese opened two ports to trade with the United States.*

Right: *Millard Fillmore, thirteenth president of the United States, brought the country one step closer to civil war by enforcing the Fugitive Slave Act of 1850.*

59

Franklin
PIERCE
1804-1869

Franklin Pierce entered the presidency with an impressive record of public service, but he proved unable to stem the tide that was inexorably dragging the nation toward civil war. The son of a New Hampshire governor, Pierce was born in Hillsboro, New Hampshire on 23 November 1804. He was graduated from Bowdoin College and was admitted to the bar in 1827. Pierce entered politics as a Democrat and made a rapid ascent from the state legislature to the United States House of Representatives and finally to the Senate. He seems to have resigned his Senate seat in 1842 on the insistence of his beloved wife, who loathed politics. He was then only 37.

Before his resignation Pierce had made a name for himself, and his political potential was probably enhanced by his service in the Mexican War during the mid-1840s. When the Democratic convention of 1852 reached a deadlock, Pierce, a Northerner with pronounced Southern sympathies, was nominated as a compromise candidate. Hearing the news of her husband's nomination, Mrs Pierce was reported to have fainted. Yet he swept the election with 254 electoral votes, compared with 42 for his opponent, General Winfield Scott. As Pierce began his administration the omens were grim. That year witnessed the publication of Harriet Beecher Stowe's novel, *Uncle Tom's Cabin*, which galvanized antislavery sentiment. Among his Cabinet appointments was Secretary of War Jefferson Davis, soon to be president of the Confederacy.

Despite gestures of impartiality, Pierce's sympathies for the South and slavery were evident. This was especially seen in his approval of the Kansas-Nebraska Act of 1854. By giving these vast territories the right to decide on slavery for themselves, the act negated the Compromise of 1850. Inevitably, a miniature civil war soon flared up in Kansas between slavery and Free-Soil partisans. What little effort Pierce made regarding 'Bleeding Kansas' were largely on the proslave side, and that bias doomed his presidency.

There were, to be sure, some successes in his administration, most notably his promotion of the idea of transcontinental railroads and the Gadsden Purchase, which bought 29,000 square miles of land from Mexico. But further discord was stimulated by what came to be called the Ostend Manifesto; pursuant to Pierce's designs on Cuba, the document proposed to annex that island, by force if necessary, if a slave revolt there threatened to spread to the South.

Pierce had attempted to reduce tensions by appeasing the South. Instead, he had allowed those tensions to move closer to the brink of civil war. His party ignored him at the 1856 convention, and Pierce retired to New Hampshire. During the Civil War, his increasingly vituperative criticism of Lincoln lost him even the affection of his own state. He died in Concord on 8 October 1869.

Left: *The first Republican Convention was held at Lafayette Hall in Pittsburgh, Pennsylvania on 22 February 1856. The new Republican Party, later nicknamed the Grand Old Party (GOP), was strongly antislavery while the Democrats continued to be split on the issue.*

Right: *Franklin Pierce, fourteenth president of the United States.*

James
BUCHANAN
1791-1868

James Buchanan arrived in the presidency as a loyal Democratic party man and a moderate. Ultimately, his very moderation made him the wrong leader for a time when centrifugal tensions were already drawing slavery and antislavery forces beyond the reach of compromise. Born in Mercersburg, Pennsylvania, on 23 April 1791, Buchanan practiced law and entered the state legislature in 1815. Following service in the United States House of Representatives and Senate and a stint as minister to Russia, he had made enough of a reputation to be mentioned as a possible Democratic presidential candidate in 1844. Polk, the winner of that election, named Buchanan secretary of state.

Perhaps the turning point in Buchanan's career came in 1854, when he was serving as President Pierce's minister to Britain. Buchanan was instrumental in drafting the Ostend Manifesto, a secret document – later leaked – that claimed the United States had the right to take Cuba by force if a slave rebellion there threatened to spread to the South. The manifesto was quickly disavowed, but it endeared Buchanan to the South. Running as the Democratic presidential candidate in 1856, Buchanan succeeded in taking every one of the slave states.

Moderate though he was, it was clear that the South was his primary constituency. In his inaugural address Buchanan proclaimed a policy of noninterference with the existing slave states and espoused local choice in the matter within the territories. Shortly thereafter the Supreme Court issued the Dred Scott Decision, stating that slaves and their descendants were not citi-

zens, but property, and that Congress had no right to deprive white citizens of such property. This decision had an incendiary effect on the nation, at once giving legal power to the South and moral strength to the new antislavery Republican party. By stoutly upholding the Fugitive Slave Law and by approving a proslavery constitution for Kansas, Buchanan did nothing to assuage the dangerous militancy now fulminating in the North.

In October 1859 came the most ominous development of all, when violent abolitionist John Brown and a small group of followers ended a murderous spree by raiding an arsenal at Harper's Ferry, Virginia, hoping thereby to seize weapons to arm slaves. Brown was captured and hanged, but his deed reverberated around the country. In the South, it raised the old fear of slave revolt. In the North, abolitionists began to speak of Brown as a saintly martyr. It was perhaps at this moment that any hope of peaceful compromise vanished. Now the fuse was in place and about to be lit, and neither Buchanan nor anyone else could stop the inevitable explosion.

The first 1860 Democratic Convention was a fiasco; failing to push through a proslavery plank, Southern delegates walked out and formed their own convention. Finally, *two* opposing Democratic candidates were nominated, a situation which allowed untried Republican Abraham Lincoln to win the election. Immediately, South Carolina seceded from the Union. In his final address to Congress, Buchanan offered no solution, saying that while states had no legal basis for secession, neither did the federal government have the right to prevent it. Buchanan retired to his estate in Pennsylvania, supporting the Union during the war. He died near Lancaster, Pennsylvania, on 1 June 1868.

Left: *Fifteenth president of the United States, James Buchanan.*

Top right: *Secession meeting in Charleston, South Carolina, in 1860.*

Above: *Capture of John Brown at Harper's Ferry.*

Abraham
LINCOLN
1809-1865

Every people needs its great leaders, its saints and its martyrs. The importance and the almost mythical presence of Abraham Lincoln in American history results from his being all those things. Rising from obscurity to lead the nation through its greatest trial, he brought to the task a nobility of character and moral courage combined with a genius for politics and for language that stirred the soul. Without someone of his stature, it is possible that the United States might have foundered.

Lincoln was born in a log cabin in Hardin, Kentucky, on 12 February 1809, the son of a barely educated frontier farmer. Seven years later, he moved with his family to Indiana. From his youth, ambition kindled in him a desire for life beyond the farm. Though he attended school for less than a year, he studied hard on his own, sometimes walking miles to borrow books. His efforts to educate himself first brought him to the Bible and historical works, later to the writings of Shakespeare and Robert Burns, and finally to the study of law. The latter began after he had moved to New Salem, near Springfield, Illinois, in 1831. Reading law while he worked at various jobs, he was admitted to the bar in 1836 and moved to Springfield to practice.

By that time, he had risen enough in the world to begin a political career. He was first elected to the Illinois house as a Whig in 1834, and he remained there until 1842. Lincoln was a competent but rather lackluster legislator, twice failing to be elected speaker of the house. By the time he left the legislature his law practice was prospering, and he was able to marry the high-spirited Mary Todd. Though Mary was to prove a difficult person at times, having more education but less breadth of mind than her husband, their marriage was largely happy. His practice as a circuit-riding lawyer brought Lincoln in contact with people of influence all

Left: *The earliest known photograph of Lincoln, taken in 1846, when he was 37 years old.*

Below: *The original log cabin in which Lincoln lived as a boy.*

Right: *Abraham Lincoln was the sixteenth president of the United States.*

over the state. Slowly, he began to be known in statewide political circles and eventually became a political power himself.

He returned to active politics by running for the United States House of Representatives. Elected in 1846 as a Whig, he managed to make little headway over the next two years, and in 1849 he returned to private life in Springfield somewhat disillusioned. Then, in 1854, something roused him again. That year his Illinois political rival, Stephen A Douglas, gained passage of the Kansas-Nebraska Act in the United States Senate. Lincoln began speaking out against the act, which allowed slavery into new territories if they so voted. Though Lincoln was personally convinced of slavery's evil, and to many his political views seemed radical, his actual position was still that of a moderate: slavery should be deplored but still temporarily protected in the South; by no means should it be allowed to extend into the territories. He was to maintain this position into the war though his antislavery bias soon became obvious.

In 1856 Lincoln joined the new antislavery Republican party and in 1858 became its nominee to challenge Douglas for the Senate. The two began a series of debates which were to make Lincoln a national figure. Lincoln challenged Douglas on his accommodations to slavery, saying, 'A house divided against itself cannot stand. I believe this government cannot endure permanently half slave and half free.' Though Lincoln lost the election he had shown himself the most dynamic and eloquent Republican leader in the country. That reputation bore fruit in 1860, when he gained the Republican nomination for president and, facing a split Democratic party, won the election. Hearing the news of the advent of this supposed anti-Southern president, seven states of the lower South seceded from the Union, and the catastrophe dreaded from the founding of the nation arrived at last.

Lincoln came to Washington an unknown, a man with only two unsuccessful years of experience in national politics. He had been elected on the strength of his antislavery position, his eloquence and such irrelevancies as being dubbed 'Honest Abe' and 'The Illinois Railsplitter.' (Lincoln later observed that he couldn't remember having split rails more than a day in his life.) In manner and appearance he was not immediately prepossessing. Despite the brilliance of his rhetoric, his voice was high and flat, his frame gaunt and awkward and his clothes ill-fitting. His face, though it

Left: *Lincoln's law office in Springfield, Illinois in 1858 was above the shop at the end of the block.*

Right: *The fifth debate between Lincoln and Douglas was held at Galesburg, Illinois, on 7 October 1858.*

Below: Honest Abe Taking Them on the Half Shell. *This campaign cartoon of 1860 plays on Lincoln's nicknames, 'Honest Abe' and 'The Railsplitter,' and on Lincoln and the Republicans taking advantage of the split in the Democratic Party.*

Overleaf: *President Lincoln writing the Proclamation of Freedom.*

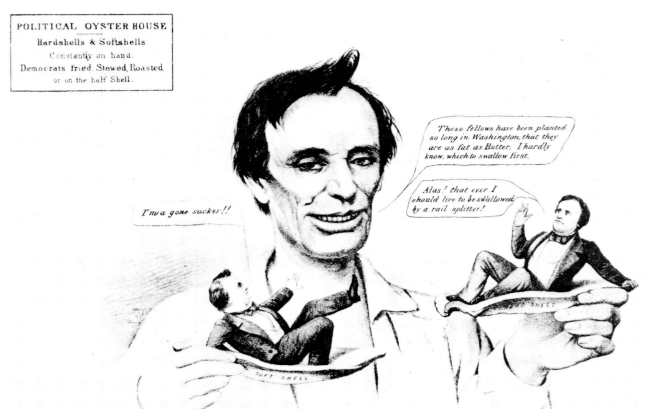

WITHOUT SLAVERY THE WAR WOULD NOT
AND WITHOUT SLAVERY
IT WOULD NOT BE CONTINUED.
MAP of EUROPE
CALL
PETITION
PROTEST
MEMORIAL from the U.P. CHURCH
PROTECTION from RAIDS
DEMOCRATIC RESOLUTIONS
FROM J.B. FLOYD Asking to be EXCHANGED
MEMORIAL from the QUAKERS
TO ALTER CONSTITUTION
HELPER
UNCLE TOM
COURT
HISTORY of the UNITED STATES
WORLD
PROTEST FROM ARMY OF POTOMAC AGAINST GUARDING PROPERTY of TRAITOR

had unmistakable nobility, looked as though it were hewn with an axe, and a scrubby new growth of whiskers did not help. Perhaps worst of all, he had the disconcerting habit of cracking jokes at the most inappropriate times, as if he were sitting around with his cronies in Illinois. A member of his cabinet dismissed him as 'the original gorilla.' Unsophisticated as he was, he seemed an unlikely man to save the Union.

In his inaugural address Lincoln made a succinct statement of his position: 'In your hands, my dissatisfied fellow countrymen, and not in mine is the momentous issue of civil war.' He would not attack the South or challenge slavery there, but he would at all costs preserve the Union. He ended the address with a typically Lincolnesque peroration: 'The mystic chords of memory will yet swell the chorus of the Union, when again touched, as they surely will be, by the better angels of our nature.'

Left: *Photograph of Lincoln by Mathew Brady, 23 February 1861.*

Below: *The Confederates attacked Fort Sumter on 12 April 1861, beginning the Civil War.*

Right: *Lincoln on the Antietam battlefield, shortly after the bloodiest day's fighting of the war.*

Overleaf: *The fall of Petersburg in 1865 marked the end of the Civil War.*

His first test was the problem of Fort Sumter, a Federal garrison in South Carolina's Charleston Harbor that was claimed and surrounded by the Confederacy. Showing the political acumen that he would demonstrate many times again, Lincoln neither evacuated nor reinforced the garrison, but declared his intention to send it supplies. He thereby made sure that the beginning of hostilities would be the South's responsibility. And so it happened: the South attacked Sumter on 12 April 1861, and the war began.

Lincoln's response, taken independently since Congress was in recess, was swift and dramatic. Assuming virtually dictatorial powers, he proclaimed a blockade of Southern ports, called for 75,000 volunteers to suppress the rebellion, suspended the privilege of habeas corpus for political suspects, and made massive expenditures without appropriations. In the wake of these actions, four more Southern states seceded.

The border states of Kentucky, Maryland and Missouri had not yet seceded, but they were slaveholding states of divided sentiment. Again showing his genius for political strategy, Lincoln managed to secure first their neutrality and finally their loyalty. When Congress returned in July 1861, it found the new president firmly in control. Over the next four years relations between Congress and Lincoln would be strained, with opinion in Washington boiling, as everywhere else, with vitriolic factions. Some would call Lincoln a bloodthirsty tyrant, and others, a cowardly conciliator. But Lincoln stood up to Congress, his recalcitrant Cabinet and public opinion, leaving them to mind their own affairs and keeping them from meddling in his business. In the end, he was to earn the admiration and loyalty of most of the North and many of his former enemies.

For some time the Union's military organization was sadly disorganized. Though he first appointed the superannuated Winfield Scott and then George B McClellan to head the Federal war effort, Lincoln took broad responsibility for directing military affairs in the first part of the war. Though his ideas were often sounder than those of his generals – he understood that enemy armies, not enemy territory, were the real target – he lacked the means to realize his strategies. As a result, the Union war effort floundered under bad generals and poor co-ordination until Lincoln appointed Ulysses S Grant to head the Army in 1864.

In 1862 Lincoln announced the Emancipation Proclamation. Though the proclamation only concerned slaves in the South and thus in reality freed none at all, it was nonetheless the beginning of the end of slavery. The proclamation transformed the war from a fight against secession to a crusade against slavery, thereby forestalling vital European recognition of the Con-

Left: *Lincoln with his family.*

Below: *Lincoln delivering his Gettysburg Address, 19 November 1863, in which he predicted 'a new birth of freedom.'*

Right: *The assassination of Lincoln at Ford's Theater, 14 April 1865.*

Below right: *Abraham Lincoln's funeral in New York City.*

federacy and galvanizing moral sentiment in the North.

As the 1864 election approached, the war was at a standstill, and it appeared that Lincoln had little chance for re-election. Running against him were two generals he had previously sacked; and his treasury secretary, Salmon P Chase, darling of the Radical Republicans who pilloried Lincoln for his conciliatory ways, also aspired to the presidency. But Lincoln neutralized Chase by keeping him in the Cabinet, and decisive Union victories in Atlanta and Mobile Bay gave Lincoln the election. On 8 April 1865, Robert E Lee surrendered at Appomattox. One week later, in the midst of plans for reconstruction, Lincoln was assassinated by a Southern fanatic, John Wilkes Booth.

Though he has made his share of mistakes, Lincoln had led the nation through its agony better than anyone else imaginable. In his Gettysburg Address and his second inaugural address, he explained the war as a great and inescapable purification struggle for North and South alike: 'With malice toward none, with charity for all . . . let us strive on to finish the work we are in, to bind up the nation's wounds . . . to do all which may achieve a just and lasting peace among ourselves and with all nations.' The final tragedy of his death was that it left that great task to lesser men.

Andrew
JOHNSON
1808-1875

Though he never attended school and began his career as a tailor, Andrew Johnson raised himself to high political office. His fortunes came to a glorious climax during the Civil War and then sank to disaster when he was propelled into the presidency by Lincoln's assassination. Born in Raleigh, North Carolina on 29 December 1808, Johnson settled in Tennessee, opened a tailor shop and educated himself with the help of his wife. Discovering a talent for oratory and politics, he became Democratic mayor of Greenville in

1830 and later a member of the Tennessee house. His tireless advocacy of the interests of small farmers, public education and free homesteads took him to the United States House of Representatives, the governorship and finally the Senate in 1857.

With the onset of secession and war came Johnson's finest moment. A slaveholder dedicated to the Union, he was the only Southern senator to support the Union in 1861. His courage was applauded throughout the North, and Lincoln named Johnson military governor of Tennessee. Acting ably in that post, Johnson restored civil government to the state before the end of the war. In a typically adroit political move, Republican Lincoln chose this Southern Democrat as his running mate on the 1864 Union ticket. Shortly after their victory, the war was won and Lincoln was dead. It was Johnson's unenviable lot to put the country back together.

Left: *On Lincoln's death, Andrew Johnson became the seventeenth president of the United States.*

Below: *Crowds jeered Johnson during his tour of the East and Mid-West in 1866.*

He started off badly at his inauguration, when he appeared drunk and ranted incoherently in his booming voice. Approaching Reconstruction as president, Johnson was not only buffeted by the conflicting demands of the Radical Republicans, his own Democrats and the still-defiant South, but he was also hamstrung by his Southern, smalltown, States' Rights and racist outlook, his inflexible personality and the sheer limitations of his intellect. It would have taken a Lincoln to steer a bold course in those times. Out of his depth, Johnson could only rail and flounder.

Events snowballed through the next years. Johnson proposed a restrained reconstruction plan, but one that failed to protect black civil rights. The South then enacted codes to disenfranchise blacks, and the Ku Klux Klan began its reign of terror. Johnson vetoed three congressional bills: the Civil Rights Bill, the First Reconstruction Act, and one expanding the authority of the Freedmen's Bureau. Congress overrode all these vetoes, virtually taking executive authority and further strengthening its hand with the Tenure of Office Act, which denied the president even the power to dismiss officials appointed or approved by Congress.

In August 1867 Secretary of War Stanton informed Johnson that military governors of the South were to be answerable to Congress and not to the president. At that point of nearly final usurpation of executive authority, Johnson took his stand. In defiance of the Tenure of Office Act, he fired Stanton. After heated clashes between Johnson and Congress, this stand led to an unprecedented confrontation: Congress initiated impeachment proceedings against the president. The reasons cited were a mélange of charges, most of which were dubious and some patently false, ostensibly adding up to 'high crimes and misdemeanors.' The principle issue, however, was Johnson's firing Stanton. As the nation held its breath, Congress took the critical vote on 16 March 1868. Because seven Republicans joined the pro-Johnson forces, impeachment was averted by one vote. (Those Republicans were men of courage; their vote reflected a very real fear that impeachment would permanently cripple the presidency. The political careers of all seven were thereby irreversibly ruined, as they knew would happen.)

Johnson left office a defeated and supremely bitter man, having only two successes to his credit: buying Alaska from Russia and helping remove French forces from Mexico. Nonetheless, he doggedly re-entered politics and, shortly before his death, was elected to the Senate. He died in Tennessee on 31 July 1875.

Below: *This 1867 view of the Reconstruction proved fanciful; in fact, the South failed to adjust to the Emancipation.*

Right: *Congressmen Thaddeus Stevens and John A Bingham before the Senate during impeachment proceedings against Johnson.*

HARPER'S WEEKLY.
A JOURNAL OF CIVILIZATION

VOL. XII.—No. 585.]　　　NEW YORK, SATURDAY, MARCH 14, 1868.　　　[SINGLE COPIES, TEN CENTS.
$4.00 PER YEAR IN ADVANCE.

Entered according to Act of Congress, in the Year 1868, by Harper & Brothers, in the Clerk's Office of the District Court of the United States, for the Southern District of New York.

IMPEACHMENT—THADDEUS STEVENS AND JOHN A. BINGHAM BEFORE THE SENATE.—Sketched by Theodore R. Davis.—[See Page 163.]

Ulysses Simpson
GRANT
1822-1885

One of the towering military leaders in American history and the man who took the Union to victory in the Civil War, Ulysses S Grant arrived in the presidency as one of the most celebrated men in the world. Such was the respect Grant held that even after two terms rocked by scandals and lacking in clear and competent leadership, he left office with his prestige scarcely dimmed.

Grant was born the son of a leather tanner in Point Pleasant, Ohio, on 27 April 1822. He was baptized Hiram Ulysses. Though as a youth he showed no special talents, his father got him an appointment to West Point. Arriving at the academy, Hiram discovered that his name appeared on the rolls as Ulysses Simpson

Grant, and he went along with the change. After four lonely years, he was graduated in 1843, having distinguished himself in little but horsemanship.

Grant deplored the Mexican War as a blatant land grab, but while participating in it, he showed proficiency at commanding troops. When the war ended, in 1848, he married Julia Dent, and their relationship was to remain unusually close throughout his life. At the outset, however, their closeness nearly cost him his military career. Posted on the West Coast, Grant, lonely for his wife, took to drink and in 1854 resigned in some disgrace. After several years of poverty and failure, he moved to Galena, Illinois, to work for his father.

His resurrection came in the form of the Civil War, during which this chronic failure and occasionally extravagant drinker, who was also a gentle and sensitive man who hated the sight of blood, discovered the one thing on earth he was good at: leading large numbers of men in acts of mayhem and death. Gaining a Union Army commission, Grant found fame with his capture of Confederate Forts Henry and Donelson. His terse

Left: *After a successful military career during the Civil War, Ulysses S Grant was elected eighteenth president of the United States.*

Below: *The capture of Fort Donelson was one of Grant's Civil War triumphs.*

Right: *Grant was known to have a penchant for smoke and drink. This 1872 cartoon depicts him as a tipsy Bowery bum.*

Far right: *Grant's political inexperience laid him open to corruption. Not only the executive branch was riddled with fraud; in New York City the Tweed Ring, supported by Tammany Hall, defrauded the city of millions of dollars. This 1872 cartoon from* Harper's Weekly *bore the caption, 'Can The Law Reach Him? ("Boss" Tweed Defying the Law).'*

note to the commander of Donelson, 'No terms except immediate and unconditional surrender can be accepted,' gained him the nickname 'Unconditional Surrender Grant.' At Donelson, and then in his historic campaign at Vicksburg, he simply swallowed enemy armies whole. From those triumphs he went on to yet another victory at Chattanooga, raising his besieged forces to chase the Confederates into Georgia. Finally Lincoln gave Grant command of the entire Union war effort in 1864. After a year of bloody hammering, Grant finally exhausted Robert E. Lee and the war was over.

In 1868 Grant easily won the presidency for the Republicans. It was not an easy time to be president. In the South, blacks were being disenfranchised and terrorized after their years of great hope. Out West, the Indians, tired of waiting for a semblance of justice and honesty from Washington, were becoming increasingly militant. And around the country the burgeoning industrial age was both threatening to destabilize the economy and giving rise to new forms of social conflict.

Grant, so decisive on the battlefield, found himself out of his element in the White House. He appointed a Cabinet of cronies and big political contributors. They formed a government of neglect, one that quickly attracted dishonest men who sensed an easy mark. The first financial disaster to hit was the Crédit Mobilier scandal of 1872, which tarnished Grant's name but did not deny him re-election. In his second term there was scandal all around him. Among other things, his private secretary was indicted as part of the Whiskey Ring and his secretary of war was caught in schemes to defraud the Indian Agency. Although Grant was entirely honest, beyond that he had little understanding of money matters and was blindly loyal to corrupt friends. Each time a friend was indicted, Grant supported him, even at the expense of his own authority.

Blacks and Indians were left to the mercy of their enemies and predators, and the captains of finance began their greatest period of aggrandizement, a process that by the end of the century would leave seven-eighths of the country's wealth in the hands of one percent of the population. Grant's one major foreign policy effort, an attempt to annex Santo Domingo, was a failure.

Passed over by his party for a third term in 1876, Grant went on a global tour, finding himself celebrated in the remotest corners of the earth. He returned to fail again to gain the nomination and in later years was swindled out of his last pennies by a friend. His *Memoirs*, one of the great military biographies, was written to recoup his fortune. He finished it a few days before he died of throat cancer on 23 July 1885, at Mount McGregor, New York. His dazzling four years during the Civil War had sufficed to carry his glory to the end of an otherwise undistinguished career of leadership, perhaps for the simple reason that without those four years the Union would have had no need of leaders at all.

Rutherford Birchard
HAYES
1822-1893

History has never quite decided on the quality of Rutherford B Hayes' presidency. But two things are clear: that Hayes was a good and honest man, almost to a fault, and that he won the presidency in one of the most bizarre elections in American history. Born in Delaware, Ohio, on 4 October 1822, Hayes was graduated from Harvard Law School in 1845. Both his law practice and political ambitions were interrupted by the Civil War; Hayes enlisted and became a major general of volunteers. Before a year was out he was in the United States House of Representatives and thereafter was three times elected governor of Ohio.

His last gubernatorial campaign, in 1875, brought Hayes national attention as an able, moderately reformist administrator, and a hard-money advocate. Not quite aware of what they were in for, the Republicans nominated Hayes for the 1876 presidential race. The troubles began when the votes were counted: Democrat Samuel J Tilden won the popular vote but electoral votes from three Southern states gave Hayes the edge in the electoral college. Instantly the Democrats cried foul, the country was in an uproar and a special electoral commission was formed. When Hayes promised to withdraw occupation troops from the South, Southern Democrats ceased their objections and the committee, voting strictly along party lines, proclaimed Hayes the victor. He was immediately dubbed 'His Fraudulency' and his election 'The Great Swap.'

Undaunted, President Hayes plunged into further controversy. Having ended Reconstruction by honoring his pledge to withdraw troops from the South, he began to work doggedly to remove patronage from government appointments and institute a merit-based procedure. This initiative was strenuously resisted by patronage dispensers in both parties, and Hayes thereby lost his power base. Yet he scored some successes, most notably in ousting the darling of the New York bosses from his powerful job as customs collector in the city (the person in question was future president Chester A Arthur). Hayes' struggle for civil service reform made only modest headway, but it did at least underline the need for reform.

Hayes was slightly more successful in his efforts to establish sound fiscal policies, turn back congressional challenges to presidential authority, and improve schooling for black Americans. Yet it was an uphill battle, and his shaky popularity in Washington was not helped by his wife, a teetotaler who refused to serve liquor in the White House and was dubbed 'Lemonade Lucy' by resentful politicos. Hayes had pledged not to seek re-election and duly left office in 1881 after one term. His later years were devoted to various humanitarian and reform efforts. He died in Fremont, Ohio, on 17 January 1893. Hayes had been an honest and earnest reformer, hampered mainly by his inability to retain the strings of power and pull them firmly. Nonetheless, he is remembered as a better than average president.

Left: *The disputed election of 1876: the commission in session. Congress appointed an electoral commission of fifteen men, eight Republicans and seven Democrats, to make the final decision. Hayes, the Republican candidate, won.*

Right: *Rutherford B Hayes, nineteenth president of the United States, attacked the patronage system and helped the country to regain commercial prosperity.*

James Abram
GARFIELD
1831-1881

The career of James A Garfield was one of the most varied of all the presidents. As a young man he trained himself for the ministry, but then commanded armies in the field, became a power in Congress and finally ended, as president, the victim of his own outmoded attachment to political patronage. Garfield was born in a log cabin in Cuyahoga County, Ohio, on 19 November 1831, the son of a poor and pious mother who saw that he attended Williams College to prepare for the ministry. By 1859, Garfield had, to the dismay of his mother, entered politics as an antislave Republican. Enlisting in the Union army during the Civil War, he fought in several important battles and rose to the rank of major general of volunteers.

While still in military service, Garfield ran for Congress and was elected to the House of Representatives in 1862. He remained at that post for the next 17 years, becoming a conservative ally of the Radical Republicans. With his middle-of-the-road style, his patience and his generous personality, Garfield gradually became a major force in Washington.

In 1880, he went to the Republican Convention as campaign manager for Senator John Sherman. There

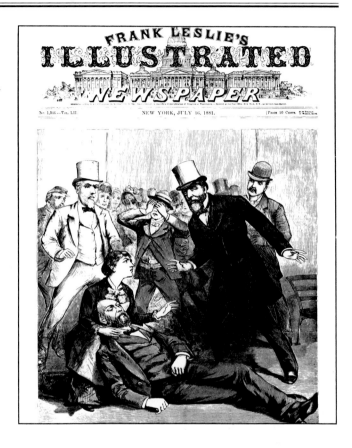

Left: *The twentieth president of the United States, James Garfield.*

Below: *Garfield is greeted by his vice-president, Chester A Arthur, on his arrival in Albany, New York, in the 1880 presidential election.*

Top right: *On 2 July 1881 Garfield was on his way to Williams College in Massachusetts when he was shot in the back by Charles J Guiteau, a disappointed office-seeker. A victim of the petty politics of the day, Garfield died several weeks later.*

his triumph and his fate came together. Working astutely behind the scenes, Garfield scuttled both the nomination of former president Ulysses S Grant, whose faction was called the 'Stalwarts,' and that of James G Blaine, leader of the so-called 'Half-Breeds.' The convention thereupon deadlocked, and on the 36th ballot, Garfield unexpectedly found himself nominated as a 'dark horse.' As a sop to the Stalwart faction, Chester A Arthur was thrown in as vice-president. In the election, Garfield defeated war hero Winfield Scott Hancock by a few thousand votes.

His predecessor in office, Hayes, had challenged the patronage system, but Garfield proceeded to exercise it to the hilt. In the process he aroused the wrath of the Stalwarts and their leader, Senator Roscoe Conkling, by two of his appointments, thus exacerbating resentments left over from the shady machinations of the convention. Passions over patronage came to a head on 2 July 1881 when, after a few months of office, Garfield was shot by Charles J Guiteau, who shouted that he was a Stalwart and wanted to make Arthur president. Garfield, fatally wounded, lingered for 11 weeks before dying on 19 September 1881.

Chester Alan
ARTHUR
1829-1886

Not surprisingly, those who have been catapulted into office by the death of a president have been a highly variable lot. When Chester A Arthur came to the presidency by that route he at least proved not to be the disaster that many observers predicted. The son of an Irish immigrant, Arthur was born in Fairfield, Vermont, on 5 October 1829. He was admitted to the New York bar in 1854. A genial and fashionable man and a hard worker, Arthur joined the Republican party at its inception and rose steadily in New York politics. During the Civil War he was an effective quartermaster general for the state. At the conclusion of the war, he helped Senator Roscoe Conkling build a Republican political machine and was rewarded by being named Collector of New York, in which position he handled the better part of the entire country's tariff revenue.

This position more or less mandated a certain level of corruption and general larceny, but Arthur balanced the requirements of the law and of his machine well enough to forge an unusually efficient operation before he was removed from the post during President Hayes' attack on patronage. Remaining a major figure in the Conkling machine and in New York politics, Arthur was nominated vice-president in the 1880 Republican Convention. (He was on the ballot to placate Conkling's 'Stalwarts,' who had seen their man Ulysses S Grant lose the nomination.) When Garfield was shot by a crazed Stalwart a few months after taking office, there was considerable trepidation about Arthur's longstanding relations with the corrupt Conkling-Stalwart machine. As one observer cracked, Arthur's civil service policy was to 'gobble all the vacancies for his particular friends and to talk reform at every gobble.'

In Arthur's inaugural address he vowed to put patronage loyalties behind him. To everyone's astonishment, he did just that. He distanced himself from Conkling, signed (albeit grudgingly) the landmark Pendleton Civil Service Reform Act of 1883 and made his appointments largely on merit. Arthur became so independent from his machine – at one point tangling directly with them on post-office reform – that he lost Stalwart support for his next presidential bid; the 1884 Republican nomination went to his old enemy James G Blaine. Already fatally ill, Arthur retired from politics and died in New York on 18 November 1886. He had taken some steps to relieve the Republican party of the corruptions of patronage. By the same token he had weakened the party, allowing a Democrat to win the presidency for the first time since before the Civil War.

Left: *Chester A Arthur, twenty-first president of the United States.*

Right: *This 1882 cartoon pokes fun at President Arthur's frequent fishing trips.*

Above: *Arthur (depicted in this* Puck *cartoon) had to deal with serious Republican party schisms during his presidency.*

Grover
CLEVELAND
1837-1908

The only man to serve two separate terms as president, Grover Cleveland might have been better off resting on the laurels of his first term, when his efficient and honest style were equal to the tasks the country faced. Cleveland was born in Caldwell, New Jersey, on 18 March 1837, the son of a poor and hard-working minister. Though he did not attend college, he studied law and began practice in Buffalo, New York, in 1859. During the Civil War he entered politics as a Democrat. His reputation for honesty and his independence from the political machines of the state helped him to be elected mayor of Buffalo and, in 1882, governor of New York.

Left: Grover Cleveland, the twenty-second and twenty-fourth president of the United States, is the only president to have been re-elected after being defeated as an incumbent.

Below: *This engraving from Harper's Weekly shows Cleveland campaigning in Brooklyn, New York, during the presidential election of 1884 (Cleveland is raising his hat in the carriage on the right).*

His conspicuous success as governor took Cleveland straight to the White House in 1884, his victory over the corruption-tainted James G Blaine creating the first Democratic administration since before the Civil War (a good many Republican 'Mugwumps' had bolted to vote for him). Cleveland came to office a portly and dynamic man, publicly a model of Victorian rectitude but with a private propensity for low life and the ladies (he admitted fathering an illegitimate child). Among the main concerns of his first term was lowering tariffs, which gained him the affection of working people but estranged powerful businessmen. Cleveland carried on the process of civil service reform by extending the merit system, and he also vetoed excessive pension legislation for veterans.

In the election of 1888 Cleveland won the popular vote but because of the electoral college allocations lost the presidency to Benjamin Harrison, who had run on a promise of protectionism. Cleveland left his first term a popular and largely successful president. Four years later Cleveland beat the ineffectual Harrison and was back in the White House.

Left: *The Haymarket Square Riot of 1886. Teamster Samuel Fielden was addressing a crowd of some 1400 people in Chicago when a bomb was thrown into the midst of the police, who had just arrived to disperse the meeting. The previous night, police had fired into a crowd of strike-breaking workers.*

Right: *William Jennings Bryan defeated Grover Cleveland for the Democratic party nomination in the election of 1896.*

Left: The Greatest Curiosity of the Nineteenth Century: *cartoon on the Cleveland administration 1892-96 in* Judge, *1894. It refers to the Panic of 1893 and ensuing depression which Cleveland could not avert.*

Previous pages: *Jacob Coxey led 400 people from Ohio to Washington DC in 1894 on a march against unemployment. 'Coxey's Army' and others like it gathered to protest the government's failure to legislate in favor of working people.*

He tried to pick up where he had left off, but now the country itself was much less stable: soon the Panic of 1893 would trigger one of the worst depressions in American history. The working class was already in turmoil, rebelling at the increasing disparity of wealth, and by 1886 the American Federation of Labor had been organized. By the 1890s labor violence was widespread. Cleveland's reformism, based on government impartiality and honesty, had no means to cope with the deteriorating relations between unrestrained big business and the masses of workers. (A not untypical attitude of industrialists was that of Jay Gould, who once said, 'I can hire one half of the working class to kill the other half.')

To ease the depression, Cleveland persuaded Congress to repeal the Sherman Silver Purchase Act, putting the country firmly on a gold standard. Then, because federal gold reserves were dangerously low, he was obliged to go to financier J P Morgan and purchase vast amounts of gold. Big business thus bailed out the government. When, in 1894, the American Railway Union went on strike to protest wage cuts, Cleveland called out federal troops to suppress the strikers. Mean-

while his efforts to help workers by again lowering tariffs were stymied by Congress. He also clashed with Congress in attempting, without success, to overthrow congressional sanction of a rather shabby American takeover of Hawaii. His firm dealings with Britain concerning that country's border dispute with Venezuela were admired but did little to arrest his declining popularity.

In the end, Cleveland's fiscal policies, insensitivity to working people and basic '*avoirdupois* and cussedness' lost him the support of the country and of his own party during his second term. As would occur throughout its history, the Democratic party splintered into factions. In the Democratic Convention of 1896, free-silver advocate William Jennings Bryan stood up and proclaimed, 'You shall not press down upon the brow of labor this crown of thorns, you shall not crucify mankind upon a cross of gold!,' and the delegates roared approval. Bryan won the nomination, and the Democratic party philosophy that Cleveland had represented was lost in the tides of history. Cleveland retired to private interests, later seeing his administration's reputation rise. He died on 24 June 1908 in Princeton, New Jersey.

Benjamin
HARRISON
1833-1901

Benjamin Harrison was one of those peculiar cases: a learned and brilliant man and a superb orator who lacked the gifts that make a first-rate president. He was born in North Bend, Ohio, on 20 August 1833, the great-grandson of a signer of the Declaration of Independence, grandson of a president and son of a senator. After college, Harrison was admitted to the bar and went into the family business: Republican politics. The only digression in his career was serving in the Civil War, during which he commanded a regiment (that he raised himself) and campaigned with General Sherman in Georgia.

After the war Harrison made his mark both as a lawyer and a politician in Indianapolis. After two unsuccessful bids for the Indiana governorship he was elected to the United States Senate in 1880, where he became a powerful conservative influence. Losing his Senate seat in 1887, he went to the Republican Convention the next year as Indiana's favorite son and unexpectedly won the nomination.

The central issue of the campaign was protectionism, and Harrison ran as an avowed high-tariff man, thus cementing the emerging alliance between Republicans and big business. In the election, President Grover Cleveland won the popular vote, but Harrison won the electoral vote. He came into office with strong ideas, but he was to have little impact in the end. During his term he signed the McKinley Tariff Bill and the controversial Silver Bill of 1890, and he supported modernization of the Navy. A proponent of civil service reform, he brought Theodore Roosevelt to Washington as civil service commissioner. And several international conferences demonstrated Harrison's desire to expand American influence through peaceful means.

Yet though his efforts in foreign relations were fruitful, Harrison's domestic policy was his downfall. The rural Populist party and the labor movement were gaining strength, thanks to growing popular hostility towards both big business and high tariffs, and this anti-Republican coalition gave the Democrats control of Congress after 1890. In the election of 1892 Harrison lost to the man he had previously defeated, Grover Cleveland. He returned to legal practice in Indianapolis, where he died on 13 March 1901.

Below: *An engraving from The Graphic, 30 July 1892, showing the clash between workers and police at the Carnegie Steelworks, Homestead, Pennsylvania.*

Right: *Benjamin Harrison, twenty-third president of the United States, was the grandson of the ninth president, William Henry Harrison.*

William
McKINLEY
1843-1901

Left: *The twenty-fifth president, William McKinley.*

Above: *McKinley was accused of bowing to big business.*

Below: *The USS* Maine *was blown up in Havana Harbor in 1898.*

William McKinley was a mild, personable man and a thoroughgoing moderate, but fate decreed that during his presidency America would begin to build an empire by force. McKinley was born in Niles, Ohio, on 29 January 1843. He served as an aide to Colonel Rutherford B Hayes during the Civil War and then took up the practice of law in Ohio, gaining enough prominence to be elected to the United States House of Representatives as a Republican in 1876.

McKinley remained in Congress until 1891, proving himself an able committee man and staunch party loyalist. He emerged as a national figure in 1890 with his McKinley Tariff Bill, an acquiescence to the desire of big business for protectionism. In a wave of popular resentment against this tariff, the Democrats came to power in Congress in 1890, and McKinley lost his seat. He returned home to serve two successful terms as governor of Ohio.

With the aid of Mark Hanna, an Ohio businessman and political organizer, McKinley won the 1896 Republican nomination. McKinley's opponent, Democrat William Jennings Bryan, electrified the country with his 'Cross of Gold' speech advocating free coinage of silver, while McKinley conducted a sedate 'front-porch campaign' in Ohio, opposing Bryan on the coinage issue and

promising a return to the high tariff that President Cleveland had ended. His campaign slogan was 'Bill McKinley and the McKinley Bill.' When the votes were counted, McKinley had won handily over the silver-tongued Bryan. Predictably, he began his administration by reinstating a high tariff.

Cuban insurrections against Spain had captured public attention. Inflamed by the press as well as by hawks in Congress, the nation was now increasingly calling for war with Spain. McKinley worked steadily for a negotiated settlement, which seemed possible until the American battleship *Maine* exploded in Havana harbor in February 1898. Spain was blamed (probably incorrectly), and McKinley succumbed to popular and congressional sword-rattling. The ensuing Spanish-American War was over in five months, disorganized American forces subduing the even more disorganized Spanish. In the wake of this victory came the acquisition of Puerto Rico, Guam and the Philippines from Spain. Thus, though McKinley was far from the unalloyed imperialist Roosevelt was to be, he had made America a world power. By 1899, Hawaii and Samoa had been annexed, and the next year American soldiers went to China to help suppress the Boxer Rebellion.

BUFFALO **EXPRESS.**

STABLISHED 1846. Vol. LVI. No. 20C.   BUFFALO, N. Y., SATURDAY, SEPTEMBER 7, 1901.   TEN PAGES.

THE PRESIDENT SHOT AT THE EXPOSITION.

Above left: *Guarding insurgent prisoners in Manila, 1898. Spain gave Puerto Rico, Guam and the Philippines to the United States after the five-month Spanish-American War.*

Above: *The assassination of President McKinley by a Polish anarchist on 6 September 1901. He died a few days later at the age of 58.*

In 1900 Americans voted for imperialism by again giving the election to McKinley over Bryan. This time, McKinley's running mate was a controversial reformer and war hero named Theodore Roosevelt. McKinley had begun to change his mind about high tariffs, and at the Buffalo, New York, Pan-American Exposition he made a speech to that effect on 5 September 1901. At a public reception the next day, he was fatally wounded by a Polish anarchist named Leon Czolgosz. He died on 14 September. McKinley had been a somewhat passive, though able, president and a reluctant empire builder; his successor was to be aggressive in all things.

Theodore
ROOSEVELT
1858-1919

Of all those whom fate brought to the White House on the death of a president, Theodore Roosevelt was by far the most able, dynamic and farsighted. Indeed, so progressive was he that it is arguable he could not have gained the presidency by any means other than accident. He came to the vice-presidency in the first place because his own party had wanted to be rid of him. Taking office in the heyday of laissez-faire capitalism, Roosevelt was to become the vanguard of a new and more democratic social order.

Born into an aristocratic New York family on 27 October 1858, the asthmatic and nearsighted youth built up his strength with sports and natural history outings. Graduated from Harvard as a Phi Beta Kappa scholar in 1880, Roosevelt was already at work on the first of his many books of history. After some law study he plunged into politics as a Republican, gaining in 1882 his first of three terms in the New York state assembly. There he soon made his progressive notions evident through his work on behalf of labor and civil service reform.

His record as a reformer took Roosevelt to Washington as United States civil service commissioner in 1889. After six years in that job he was named New York City police commissioner. There he was highly successful in attacking corruption. By 1897, when President McKinley appointed him assistant navy secretary, Roosevelt had a national reputation – as a trailblazer or as a troublemaker, depending on point of view.

Left: *Theodore Roosevelt, twenty-sixth president of the United States, had enough 'cowboy' spirit to get things done. His domestic policy was progressive, his foreign policy efforts historic. Roosevelt was pivotal in making America a modern world power.*

Right: *Roosevelt (second right, standing) and his associates in the New York State Assembly, 1882. There he made a name for himself as a reformer.*

Roosevelt's main interest as a navy secretary was certainly to cause some trouble: an imperialist who looked on war as a sort of virile sport, Roosevelt chafed for 'a bit of a spar' with Spain, whose colony in Cuba was struggling for independence. In 1898, he got both war and glory in the Spanish-American War. Roosevelt raised his own cavalry regiment – called the 'Rough Riders,' though they did not fight mounted – and led them into the pages of history with their charge up Kettle Hill during the battle of San Juan. He returned from Cuba a war hero and was immediately swept into office as governor of New York State. In November 1898 he wrote wryly to a friend, 'I have played it in bull luck this summer. First, to get into the war; and then to get out of it; then to get elected.'

Below: Next!: *The Octopus, the Standard Oil Trust in 1904. Roosevelt brought big business within the reach of the law 'in the public interest.' His administration saw no less than 25 indictments of trusts.*

Right: *As Lieutenant Colonel of the First Volunteer Cavalry (the 'Rough Riders') in the Spanish-American War of 1898, Roosevelt gained a reputation as a dynamic leader.*

Above: *Part of the comic* Life *series 'The Teddyssey,' 1907. Columbia steers Roosevelt past the monopolistic Sirens John D Rockefeller, J P Morgan and Andrew Carnegie.*

Top: *Roosevelt with his children and wife Edith in 1903. The children are (l-r): Quentin, 5; Ted, 15; Archie, 9; Alice, 19; Kermit, 13; and Ethel, 11.*

As governor, Roosevelt vigorously pursued his liberal ways, to the exasperation of the state Republican machine and the business community. Finally, state Republican leaders decided to kick the upstart upstairs. They got him on the 1900 McKinley ticket as vice-president (despite the admonition of one Republican who spluttered to his cohorts, 'Don't any of you realize that there's only one life between that madman and the presidency?') Six months later, McKinley was assassinated and the 'madman' became president. The country was to call him 'Teddy,' a nickname he hated. At 42, he was the youngest president in American history.

Roosevelt took office at a time when unregulated industry had soared to new heights of affluence and arrogance. The result was a perilous split in American society. The captains of business had prospered as never before, and the working class was poorer, more abused and angrier than ever before. It was Roosevelt's vision and his forcefulness in action that began the process of changing from laissez-faire to regulated capitalism. He began by attacking the powerful trusts. Using as his

legal weapon the Sherman Antitrust Act, he first managed to break up Morgan and Rockefeller's huge Northern Securities Company, and in dozens of subsequent 'trustbusting' efforts, Roosevelt successfully challenged the most powerful business interests in the country. Observing the results, one ironic observer wrote, 'Wall Street is paralyzed at the thought that a president . . . would sink so low as to try to enforce the law.' By no means antibusiness, Roosevelt wished less to destroy large commercial entities than to keep them under scrutiny and regulation. To that end he persuaded Congress to create the Cabinet-level Department of Commerce and Labor. In 1902 he won the further approval of labor by arbitrating an end to the United Mine Workers' strike.

But these were only part of the extraordinarily far-reaching and decisive initiatives of Roosevelt's presidency. His foreign policy efforts, though not always strictly above-board, were historic. Roosevelt had been an unalloyed imperialist who came into office preaching, 'Speak softly and carry a big stick.' Once in power, however, he toned down his dreams of an American empire in favor of international stability. In 1905, he mediated the end of the Russo-Japanese War, for which he won the Nobel Prize, and with his blessing, Japan became a world power.

When in 1903 Colombia rejected the idea of a canal in its Panamanian territory, Roosevelt encouraged a revolution that gained independence for Panama and the canal for America. At the same time he issued the 'Roosevelt Corollary' to the Monroe Doctrine, in effect making America the watchdog and policeman of the Western Hemisphere. As progressive in race relations as in other areas, Roosevelt during his first term denounced lynching and tried to establish a biracial Republican organization in the South. This outraged Southern leaders, who were then in the process of disenfranchising blacks. Fearful of losing further support in the South, Roosevelt for once backed off, and American blacks lost their last real chance for decades.

Re-elected in 1904 by the largest popular majority to date, Roosevelt proclaimed his 'Square Deal' program, which led to an impressive body of legislation despite the growing resistance of the old guard in his party. The Hepburn Act of 1906 regulated the railroads; the Pure Food and Drug Act likewise controlled the food industry. Having supported the Democrats' Newlands Act of 1902, which created extensive irrigation projects, Roosevelt went on to be a great conserver of lands, reorganizing the Forest Service and multiplying the extent of national parks and preserves fivefold. In 1907 he showed off American might by sending the Great

Left: *The sinking of Russian ship* Variag *in the Russo-Japanese War. Roosevelt won the 1905 Peace Prize for mediating the end of the war.*

Previous pages: *'Teddy' and the Rough Riders, 1898.*

Above: *US and Japanese officers pose on the deck of the* USS Missouri *in Japan, 1908.*

Right: *A late photograph of Theodore Roosevelt.*

White Fleet on a world cruise.

Roosevelt left the presidency to his chosen successor, Taft, in 1909. He was at that point beloved by the majority of his countrymen but estranged from conservatives in his party. A bid for the Republican nomination in 1912 failed. He then ran on the Progressive ('Bull Moose') ticket, thereby splitting the vote and insuring the election of Woodrow Wilson. Roosevelt died on 6 January 1919, from the malarial after-effects of a South American expedition. Had he lived, he might well have won a nomination in 1920. As it was, with him died America's most extraordinary exemplar of progressive Republicanism. Though Roosevelt had by no means forged all his more radical ideas into law, many of those ideas would be the inspiration of progressive legislation for decades to come.

William Howard
TAFT
1857-1930

William Howard Taft was a man who hated politics yet spent most of his life in that profession, a man virtually without ambition who was appointed to many important offices but who was elected only to one: the presidency.

Taft was born in Cincinnati, Ohio, on 15 September 1857, and attended law school after graduating from Yale. He practiced law for a few years before being appointed to various judgeships including the circuit court. By 1900 Taft had become prominent enough in Republican politics to be appointed civil governor of the Philippines. During his four years there he helped bring peace to that troubled new American possession. When Roosevelt became president, he named Taft secretary of war. In the cabinet, Taft became a close advisor of the president and finally his chosen successor. Thus, in 1908, Taft won the Republican nomination, and in the election he easily defeated perennial Democratic candidate William Jennings Bryan.

Within Taft's prodigious figure – he weighed upwards of 300 pounds – lay a brilliant if conventional mind; but he was a reluctant politician and a plodding and colorless administrator, a striking contrast to his electric predecessor. More conservative than Teddy Roosevelt, he nonetheless actively carried on the trustbusting (he signed the landmark Sherman Antitrust Act of 1890) and the conservation efforts of his mentor and was generally supportive of the labor movement. In foreign relations, Taft promoted the idea of 'dollar diplomacy,' using economic rather than military power to spread American influence. During his tenure, the parcel post system was created, and constitutional amendments were enacted for a federal income tax and popular election of senators.

But Taft's conservatism and political fumbling finally alienated the progressive wing of the party, and Roosevelt with it. Thus in the election of 1912 Roosevelt ran against Taft with his own Republican splinter coalition, the Bull Moose party. When the electoral votes were tallied, Roosevelt had 88, Taft 8 and Democrat Woodrow Wilson 435, whereupon Taft left politics to teach at Yale. In 1921 he was appointed to the job he had wanted all along: chief justice of the Supreme Court. In his years on the court he proved to be more a capable administrator and organizer than a dynamic jurist. After a life of effective, if often subdued, public service, Taft died in Washington, DC, on 8 March 1930.

Left: *This political cartoon shows out-going President Taft gladly passing the 'Mexican problem' on to his successor Woodrow Wilson in 1913. A coup in Mexico had put a ruthless dictator, Victoriano Huerta, in power.*

Top: *Taft was a civil governor in the Philippines at the time of the Boxer Rebellion in China, 1900.*

Right: *William Taft became the twenty-seventh president of the United States in 1909. Though he continued Roosevelt's progressive domestic programs (he was particularly effective in trustbusting), he lacked the enthusiasm and resolve of his famous predecessor.*

Woodrow
WILSON
1856-1924

Destined to be one of the greatest presidents, Woodrow Wilson came into office having already achieved acclaim as both a scholar and an educator. His tenure as president was marked by great strides in social justice and tireless labors to achieve peace, yet in the end he was to be thwarted in the accomplishment of his noblest dream.

Born in Staunton, Virginia, on 28 December 1856, Wilson grew up in Georgia and the Carolinas, where his father was a Confederate chaplain. Young as he was during the Civil War, he saw enough of its horrors to become a life-long crusader for peace. After being graduated from Princeton, Wilson gained a law degree

and practiced briefly. Tiring of law, he returned to academia and took a doctorate in political science at Johns Hopkins University. His dissertation became the first of a brilliant series of books and articles on government, writings which both contributed much to the world's understanding of political systems and to their author's later mastery of statecraft.

Wilson taught at Bryn Mawr and Wesleyan (where he coached a winning football team) before going to Princeton to teach in 1890. Two years later he was appointed president of the university, and over the next eight years, he revitalized the school, in the process influencing the whole university system in the country. His chief innovations, later adopted by many leading colleges, were the preceptorial system – supplementing lectures with small study groups – and the quadrangle plan – establishing small communities of students and teachers within the university. But, like most reformers, he found at Princeton his share of enemies, and in 1910 they forced his resignation.

Left: *Woodrow Wilson served two terms as the twenty-eighth president of the United States. His second term was dominated by the outbreak of war in Europe.*

Below: *The inauguration of Wilson in 1913. The first Democratic president since Grover Cleveland, he was a successful reformer.*

They did him a favor. The now unemployed Wilson was recruited by the Democrats to run for governor of New Jersey. He won the election and soon showed that he was not the docile servant of the Democratic machine that he was supposed to be. He pushed through a number of reforms, including a direct primary law and the creation of a public utilities commission. Within two years, his performance as governor had brought him national fame, and at the 1912 Democratic Convention Wilson became a presidential nominee. Though this scholarly intellectual cut an unaccustomed figure in American politics, Wilson was a rousing campaigner, pitting his 'New Freedom' program of social reform against Roosevelt's Progressive party 'New Nationalism' and the Republicans' business-as-usual platform. Aided by the split in the opposition, Wilson won by a tremendous electoral college majority.

Once in office Wilson made good use of his years of thinking about and managing political processes. His first effort was to gain passage of the Underwood Act, which both lowered tariffs that business interests had kept high for years and imposed the nation's first graduated income tax. The same year saw the Federal Reserve Act, and next year the establishment of the Federal Trade Commission. Next came the Clayton Antitrust Act, which recognized trade unions and strikes as legal, and the landmark Adamson Act, which in mandating for railroad workers an eight-hour day,

paved the way for the extension of this right to all labor. Still later came a bill attacking child labor abuses.

Though Congress and the public proved amenable to his domestic reforms, Wilson had less luck with foreign relations. His first problem occurred with Mexico, where the Huerta government had come to power by assassination in 1913. Denying the validity of the new government, Wilson took a position of 'watchful waiting.' A series of crises ensued. Finally Wilson sent troops to occupy Veracruz, and after some tense negotiations Huerta resigned. Then Pancho Villa appeared, a new man hopeful of taking power. When Villa raided New Mexico in 1916, Wilson sent General Pershing chasing after him. Nervous about the American military presence inside her borders, Mexico came near to declaring war. Wilson called off Pershing and managed at the last minute to avoid the threat.

By then he had a far more ominous situation to contemplate: in the summer of 1914 war had broken out in Europe. Wilson was an ardent opponent of all war, believing that it brutalized the very soul of a nation.

Below: *The* Lusitania *embarking on a voyage. More than 100 Americans were drowned when the ship was torpedoed on 7 May 1915.*

Right: The New York Times *and most other daily papers of 8 May 1915 headlined the sinking of the* Lusitania.

"All the News That's
Fit to Print."

The New York Times.

EXTRA
5:30 A. M.

VOL. LXIV...NO. 20,923. ..... NEW YORK, SATURDAY, MAY 8, 1915.—TWENTY-FOUR PAGES. ONE CENT

LUSITANIA SUNK BY A SUBMARINE, PROBABLY 1,260 DEAD;
TWICE TORPEDOED OFF IRISH COAST; SINKS IN 15 MINUTES;
CAPT. TURNER SAVED, FROHMAN AND VANDERBILT MISSING;
WASHINGTON BELIEVES THAT A GRAVE CRISIS IS AT HAND

SHOCKS THE PRESIDENT

Washington Deeply Stirred by the Loss of American Lives.

BULLETINS AT WHITE HOUSE

Wilson Reads Them Closely, but Is Silent on the Nation's Course.

HINTS OF CONGRESS CALL

Loss of Lusitania Recalls Firm Tone of Our First Warning to Germany.

CAPITAL FULL OF RUMORS

Reports That Liner Was to be Sunk Were Heard Before Actual News Came.

Special to The New York Times.

WASHINGTON, May 7.— Never since that April day, three years ago, when word came that the Titanic had gone down, has Washington been so stirred as it is tonight over the sinking of the Lusitania.

The Lost Cunard Steamship Lusitania

SOME DEAD TAKEN ASHORE

Several Hundred Survivors at Queenstown and Kinsale.

STEWARD TELLS OF DISASTER

ADVERTISEMENT.

NOTICE!

TRAVELLERS intending to embark on the Atlantic voyage are reminded that a state of war exists between Germany and her allies and Great Britain and her allies; that the zone of war includes the waters adjacent to the British Isles; that, in accordance with formal notice given by the Imperial German Government, vessels flying the flag of Great Britain, or of any of her allies, are liable to destruction in those waters and that travellers sailing in the war zone on ships of Great Britain or her allies do so at their own risk.

IMPERIAL GERMAN EMBASSY
WASHINGTON, D. C., APRIL 22, 1915.

Cunard Office Here Besieged for News; Fate of 1,918 on Lusitania Long in Doubt

Nothing Heard from the Well-Known Passengers on Board—Story of Disaster Long Unconfirmed While Anxious Crowds Seek Details.

List of Saved Includes Capt. Turner; Vanderbilt and Frohman Reported Lost

Saw the Submarine 100 Yards and Watched Torpedo as

Ernest Cowper, a Toronto Newspaper Attack, Seen from Ship's Rail Used in Torpedoes, Say Others

Queenstown, Saturday, May 8, 3:18 A. M.

Left: *A rare photo of General Pershing with Mexican revolutionary Pancho Villa.*

Below: *Wilson's re-election campaign stressed his promise to keep the United States out of the war.*

Opposite, left: *Wilson campaign poster, St Louis, 1916.*

Opposite, right: *In 1917 Wilson said, 'The world must be made safe for democracy.'*

Accordingly, he made prodigious efforts not only to remain neutral but to mediate among the warring powers. When a German submarine sank the British liner *Lusitania* in 1915, killing over 100 Americans, Wilson issued a stern warning to Germany but would not budge from neutrality.

In 1916, Wilson was re-elected on the slogan 'He kept us out of war.' But in early 1917 Germany declared that she would conduct unrestricted submarine warfare, attacking American ships, if necessary, and Wilson reluctantly called for war. The declaration was passed by Congress on 6 April 1917. America's task, Wilson said, was to 'make the world safe for democracy.' After pushing through the Selective Service Act, Wilson took control of the railroads and installed Bernard M Baruch as head of the War Industries Board. Largely leaving the actual conduct of the war to Baruch and other able

hands, Wilson turned his attention to the vital question of how to maintain peace in the postwar world.

On 8 January 1918, while the war ground on in the trenches of Europe, Wilson proclaimed his Fourteen Points, an extraordinarily prescient document mandating freedom of the seas, arms reduction, an end to secret treaties and, most important, a League of Nations to settle future disputes. By November 1918, Wilson had convinced Germany to sign an armistice on the assurance that a settlement would be based on the Fourteen Points.

But, to the great detriment of future world peace, things were not to work out that way. Wilson arrived at the Versailles Peace Conference of early 1919 already an ill and exhausted man. He was outmaneuvered by the leaders of the other victorious powers – France, Italy and Great Britain – and the result was the scrapping of most

of the Fourteen Points and a grimly punitive settlement imposed on Germany. The League of Nations had been accepted at Versailles, however, and Wilson returned home to see its ratification through Congress.

The mood of Congress proved resistant to the League, and Wilson, perhaps because of his declining health, lacked his usual powers of persuasion. Then, during a cross-country swing to promote the League, Wilson collapsed and was incapacitated just when he was needed most. The results were the defeat of the League in the Senate and, soon, the defeat of the Democrats in the 1920 election. Ironically, in the same year he was awarded the Nobel Peace Prize. After a triumphant life and a tragic final defeat, Wilson retired to seclusion in Washington, dying there on 3 February 1924.

Left: *United States Liberty Bond poster of 1917.*

Below: *President Wilson marching in a Libery Loan parade.*

Right: *A meeting at the 1919 Versailles Peace Conference: (l-r) Louis Loucheur, Winston Churchill, David Lloyd George, and Bernard Baruch. Wilson won the Nobel Peace Prize for his efforts at the conference.*

Warren Gamaliel
HARDING
1865-1923

An undistinguished man with an undistinguished mind, Warren G Harding spent a political career following the path of least resistance. As it happened, that path took him finally to the White House. At least he knew his own limitations. He once remarked, 'I know how far removed from greatness I am.' In fact, he may have presided over the most corrupt administration in American history. Yet he himself was not so much dishonest as foolishly loyal to corrupt cronies.

Harding was born in Corsica, Ohio, on 2 November 1865. After unsuccessful law study and several job failures he became, in 1884, a partner in a newspaper, the Marion *Star*. In 1891, Harding married a local banker's daughter, Florence Kling De Wolfe. A strong and ambitious woman, she drove his political career onward. Soon Harding was taken up by Harry M Daugherty, an Ohio Republican kingmaker who orchestrated Harding's ascent from the Ohio legislature to lieutenant governorship. In 1914 he was elected to the United States Senate.

In his six years in the Senate, Harding accomplished nothing of significance, but during World War I, he endeared himself to Theodore Roosevelt by sponsoring an absurd and unsuccessful bill which would have allowed Roosevelt to raise a volunteer army. The grateful Roosevelt fixed on Harding as his running mate

in the next election. Then Roosevelt suddenly died, leaving a muddled Republican party that Daugherty, in the legendary 'smoke-filled room' of the convention, exploited to make Harding the nominee. Harding cleverly took advantage of popular weariness with the scholarly Wilson and his idealistic policies. Proclaiming that he and Florence were 'just plain folks,' Harding campaigned for a nebulous 'return to normalcy.' Such was the grand ambiguity of his rhetoric that he was lauded as both an opponent and proponent of the League of Nations. Yet the people perceived him as one of their own, and Harding won by a landslide over his opponent, James M Cox.

Harding made a few good Cabinet appointments, but other Cabinet members, including Daugherty, would leave a legacy of corruption. Harding was a conservative, high-tariff, pro-business, laissez-faire politician, but he was simply no administrator, preferring to play poker and drink bootleg liquor with his buddies in the White House (all the while professing his allegiance to Prohibition).

In 1923, as Washington buzzed with rumors of pending revelations, two members of Harding's inner circle committed suicide. The same year Harding set out on a transcontinental tour during which he learned that the misdeeds of his associates were about to be exposed. Shaken, he became ill and died of an embolism in San Francisco on 2 August. Shortly thereafter the Teapot Dome scandal shook the country. Among those implicated were Daugherty and two other Cabinet members. It was left to Calvin Coolidge to clean up the mess.

Opposite: *Some historians have dubbed Warren G Harding, twenty-ninth president of the United States, 'the worst president ever.'*

Top right: *The Teapot Dome scandal involved members of Harding's administration, but allegations of oil company kickbacks did not directly involve him. This cartoon shows Wilson (left) and Daugherty (right) pursued by the steamroller of the oil scandal.*

Left: *Harding and his wife Florence. Harding's imposing appearance and campaign line 'America's need is not heroics . . . but normalcy' won him a term in office.*

Calvin
COOLIDGE
1872-1933

The hands-off, pro-business style of government practiced by Calvin Coolidge may not have been very exciting, but it was well suited to the America of the 1920s. He was born in Plymouth Notch, Vermont, on 4 July 1872 and gained a law degree after attending Amherst College. Moving into Republican politics from a prosperous practice, he became mayor of Northampton, Massachusetts, and finally governor of the state in 1919.

It was during his first year as governor that Coolidge made his name and fame with a single sentence. Boston police had struck for union recognition, and Coolidge mobilized the state militia to suppress the strike, saying, 'There is no right to strike against the public safety by anybody, anywhere, any time.' The nation so applauded this sentiment that in 1920 the Republicans decided that it would be good politics to give Coolidge the vice-presidential nomination on the Harding ticket. The two swept into office.

Harding died on 2 August 1923. Recalling how he heard the news that he was to be the next president while in his father's home in Plymouth, 'Silent Cal' later reported, 'I thought I could swing it.' His father gave him the oath of office at home by lantern light. Arriving in Washington, he quickly set about organizing to insure his election in 1924. His attitudes were entirely those of conservative Republicans of the time: laissez-faire in regard to business, opposed to any sort of federal intervention on behalf of farmers and firmly in favor of governmental cost-cutting and reduced income taxes.

Coolidge once said, 'The chief business of the American people is business.' His own first order of business was to deal with the Teapot Dome scandal that the Harding administration had left behind. Coolidge cleaned house of those implicated and restored confidence in the executive branch. The country was in a period of prosperity and optimism, and on the whole Cal simply stayed out of the way. Stolid, stoic and colorless, he was just what the American people wanted: a president as withdrawn in governing as he was in manner. He was re-elected by a landslide in 1924.

Coolidge then worked successfully to reduce both taxes and the national debt. At the same time he encouraged stock market speculation that helped fuel a thrilling short-term boom but which also contributed to disaster in the future. He spent much time seeking ways of promoting international peace and helped reduce the crushing war reparations demanded of Germany. In 1928 Coolidge supported the multinational Kellogg-Briand Pact, which outlawed war. Like his encouragement of stock speculation, this well-intentioned treaty was to become moot in the tumultuous decade to come. Finally, with characteristic brevity, Coolidge simply announced, 'I do not choose to run for president in 1928.' Still much loved, he retired quietly to Northampton, writing occasional articles and an autobiography, and died there on 5 January 1933, in the midst of the Great Depression that had followed his term.

Left: *The thirtieth president of the United States, Calvin Coolidge had the task of restoring respectability to his office in the post-Harding years.*

Right: *President Coolidge (left) with Herbert Hoover, 18 July 1928. Coolidge had the good luck to serve as president during a particularly prosperous and happy time in American history; Hoover was not so fortunate.*

Herbert
HOOVER
1874-1964

A brilliant organizer and administrator who was dubbed the 'Great Engineer,' Herbert Hoover came to the presidency with immense prestige. It was, however, his fate to become one of the many victims of the Great Depression. Born to a Quaker family of West Branch, Iowa, on 10 August 1874, Hoover was graduated from Stanford University with a degree in mine engineering. He built a notable international career in that field and in 1908 set up his own company. In 1915 he took the first of several government appointments co-ordinating war relief. His work continued through and after World War I, as he orchestrated operations to feed millions of people around the war-ravaged world.

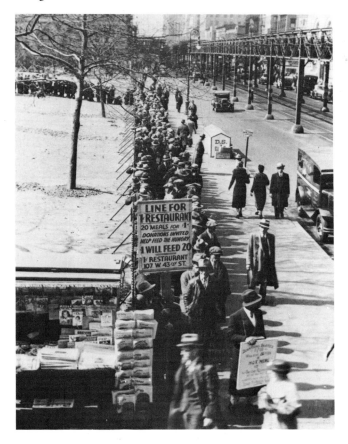

Left: *Herbert Hoover, thirty-first president of the United States, had to contend with the deepest depression the country had ever experienced.*

Above: *Breadline, 6th Avenue and 42nd Street, New York City, February 1932. Hoover's efforts to deal with the Great Depression were ineffective.*

Becoming President Harding's secretary of commerce in 1921, Hoover stayed in that position through the Coolidge administration. As secretary, his efforts were far-reaching and decisive. He mostly used voluntary co-operation to harmonize the work of manufacturing concerns around the country. Among the tangible results were the St Lawrence Seaway and the Boulder (later Hoover) Dam. Such were his success and prominence that he was nominated for president on the second ballot of the 1928 Republican Convention. Running on a platform that promised to widen existing prosperity ('a chicken in every pot, a car in every garage'), to promote relief for farmers, to enact protective tariffs and to continue Prohibition, he swamped the Democratic contender, Al Smith.

President Hoover had just begun to guide his programs through Congress when, on 29 October 1929, the roof fell in: the stock market crashed, and the country entered the bleakest depression of its history. At that point of major financial and social disaster, Hoover's philosophy of voluntarism and his avoidance of government regulation failed to find its past success. Believing the Depression would solve itself if he cut taxes and stimulated business, Hoover took little other direct action. But the enormity of the disaster was such that the nation could not afford to wait for Hoover's remedies to take effect. Around America the breadlines formed, and the wandering jobless built ramshackle settlements which they called 'Hoovervilles.' When a group of veterans camped in Washington demanding payment of bonuses, Hoover called in federal troops and had them thrown out. His useful foreign initiatives, such as an important naval limitations treaty and the Good Neighbor policy toward Latin America, could not offset his declining credibility. Though the Depression was certainly not his doing, Hoover was the man in charge, and the nation blamed him.

Finally accepting the need for direct government action, Hoover set up the Reconstruction Finance Corporation, a precursor of the New Deal. But he was too late. In the 1932 election the nation turned to a more dynamic leader with fresher ideas. Franklin D Roosevelt won by a landslide. Hoover then commenced a new career that filled the rest of his long life, writing on government matters and, in the 1940s and 1950s, chairing the 'Hoover Commissions' that helped restructure the executive department. Having lived long enough to see history somewhat exonerate his administration, Hoover died in New York on 20 October 1964. As president, he was the right man at the wrong time.

Franklin Delano
ROOSEVELT
1882–1945

One of the most controversial presidents (the 22nd Amendment, limiting a president to two terms, was inspired by his years in office), Franklin Delano Roosevelt is also one of the presidential giants. Not only did he serve much longer than any other president, but he led the country during two of its most extreme crises: the worst depression in modern times and the worst war of all time. But that is the public figure, the Roosevelt of history texts. What intrigued both his admirers and enemies was that this scion of a patrician family became known as the true friend of the American masses.

Roosevelt was born on 30 January 1882 at Hyde Park, New York, the descendant of a Dutchman who had come to New Amsterdam (later New York) in the 1640s. Roosevelt's father was a wealthy railroad executive, and his mother, a Delano, was a member of another rich New York family. Young Franklin was educated by governesses and private tutors, taking almost yearly trips to Europe with his family. But this child of privilege was by no means indulged. His father instilled in him a sense of responsibility that befit his position, while his mother was exceedingly strict (and remained a domineering presence in his life until her death). At 14 Roosevelt went to Groton, an exclusive private boys' boarding school, and then to Harvard College. He arrived there as a rather private, shy person, but through participation in sports and extracurricular activities – especially the college newspaper – he became more gregarious. How-

Above: *Franklin Delano Roosevelt, aged 12, with his mother.*

Left: *Roosevelt was born at Crum Elbow, Hyde Park, New York, in 1882.*

Right: *Franklin D Roosevelt, thirty-second president of the United States, served an unprecedented three terms in office. His optimism and resolve hauled the country out of the Depression and guided it through the trauma of World War II.*

128

Top left: *Roosevelt in 1913 as assistant secretary of the Navy.*

Left: *The Roosevelts at Hyde Park, New York, July 1932.*

Above: *Governor of New York Franklin Roosevelt with Lieutenant Governor Herbert Lehman in 1930.*

ever, he was no scholar, and though after graduation he attended Columbia University Law School, he never bothered to take a degree. Instead, he simply took the state bar exams and went to work in a New York City law firm. By this time he had married his distant cousin, Eleanor Roosevelt (a niece of Franklin's fifth cousin, Theodore Roosevelt, who was currently president). She was a woman who would become an important public figure in her own right.

Roosevelt soon realized that he was dissatisfied as a lawyer, and he eagerly accepted when he was asked by the Democratic party to run for the New York senate in 1910. He proceeded to win a seat that the Republicans had held for over 50 years. In the senate he quickly established himself as a deft yet independent politician, and after supporting Woodrow Wilson in the 1912 presidential election – against his cousin Theodore – he was rewarded with the post of assistant secretary of the navy, a job Roosevelt enjoyed because he was interested in naval history as well as in sailing. During World War I, Roosevelt became widely respected for his ability to produce results, and he was nominated by the Democrats as their vice-presidential candidate for the 1920 election. He and his running mate, James Cox, lost to Harding and Coolidge, but Roosevelt appeared to be a man with a bright future.

In August 1921, Roosevelt suddenly came down with polio after falling into the cold water off Campobello Island, his family's summer home. After months of severe pain and the threat of total paralysis, if not death, Roosevelt ended up without the use of the lower half of his body. He tried to build up his strength as much as possible by exercises and swimming, and although he would always need some support – braces, crutches and helping arms – he did regain some mobility. Although it was assumed that he would retire from an active political life, he continued to maintain his political contacts. He made a symbolic comeback in 1924 when he nominated Governor Alfred E Smith of New York at the Democratic National Convention, and although Smith failed to gain the nomination, Roosevelt emerged as a courageous crusader, for Smith was a Roman Catholic and at the time it seemed unthinkable to many that he could be president. In 1928, Smith did gain the nomination – again with Roosevelt's backing – and he persuaded Roosevelt to run for governor of New York. Smith lost to Hoover, but Roosevelt won. His political career was now well back on course.

As a two-term governor of New York, 1929–33, Roosevelt effected many administrative reforms and initiated progressive legislation. In 1932 Roosevelt ran for the presidency, and by promising to help 'the forgotten man,' he won the nomination and went on to defeat the incumbent, Herbert Hoover. In his acceptance speech at the convention, the first given by any

Top left: *Roosevelt visiting an orthopedic hospital in Seattle, Washington, during his 1932 western campaign trip.*

Below left: *FDR signing the Farm Credit Act, 16 June 1933. In his first hundred days in office he acted decisively to combat the Depression, giving America a 'new deal.'*

Above: *The Civilian Conservation Corps (CCC) demolishing an old railroad trestle in Washington state.*

Right: *CCC enrollees at soil conservation work.*

Below: *Diagram of Tennessee Valley Authority (TVA) water control system.*

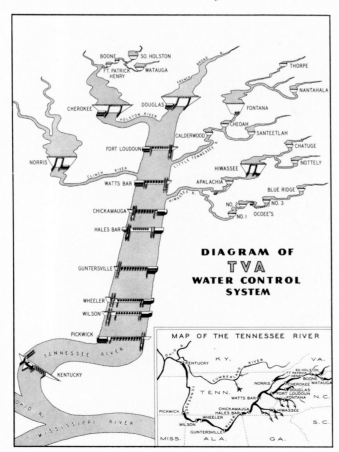

nominee in person, Roosevelt announced he would work for 'a new deal' for the American people.

Roosevelt was inaugurated on 4 March 1933, and within 48 hours he moved decisively to stem the panic 'run' on the nation's banks by declaring a 'bank holiday.' Then, on 9 March, Congress began a special session. Within 99 days (although it would come to be known as 'The Hundred Days'), it passed some of the most significant laws and reforms in the nation's history. In addition to dealing with the most immediate crises – cutting back on the federal payroll and veterans' pensions and reforming the nation's currency, finances and banks – and the 'mid-level' problems – providing funds for relief for the desperately poor, jobs on public work projects and new terms for farmers, industries and home mortgage holders – Roosevelt and his supportive Congress established a number of institutions that would remain permanent fixtures of American society. One such was the Tennessee Valley Authority (TVA), a vast undertaking involving many dams that would produce cheap electricity, thereby developing a largely neglected region. Another was the National Labor Relations Act, which gave workers and the labor movement greater rights. The Securities and Exchange Commission was set up to regulate the stock market and protect investors. Perhaps the most familiar of all was the establishment of Social Security to provide pensions for the elderly.

Left: *Election campaign for Roosevelt. He carried forty-six states in 1936; his pragmatic polices appealed to the people.*

Above: *A caricature of FDR from 1934.*

Top right: *Well-known photo of FDR in the late 1930s.*

Right: *Roosevelt won a third term on an antiwar platform, but in 1940 he was already moving from 'neutrality' to a policy of 'non-belligerency,' or open support of the Allies.*

Roosevelt's critics accused him of introducing socialism, even communism, to the country, but historians would point out later that in fact he had saved the capitalist system. Certainly he kept the nation from taking one of the extreme routes followed by other countries at this time – for instance fascist Germany and communist Russia. Just as important as his many tangible reforms was the fact that Roosevelt had helped Americans overcome what he described in his first inaugural address as the 'fear [of] fear itself.' Many of his specific agencies, laws and policies failed to eliminate the deep problems of the Depression, but Roosevelt kept the nation from disintegrating.

In September 1939 World War II began in Europe. Most Americans had little desire to become involved in another war, but Roosevelt carefully managed to provide support to the embattled British, trading them ships for bases, providing easy loans and allowing American ships to fire on German ships to protect British convoys. By the time the Japanese attacked Pearl Harbor, Roosevelt was ready to lead the United States into a full-scale war. For the remaining 52 months of his life, he played a dominant role in directing military forces and inspiring the civilian efforts of the Allies.

The New York Times.

"All the News That's Fit to Print."

LATE CITY EDITION

VOL. LXXXIX. No. 30,126. NEW YORK, THURSDAY, JULY 18, 1940. THREE CENTS

ROOSEVELT RENOMINATED ON FIRST BALLOT; STRICT ANTI-WAR PLATFORM IS ADOPTED; NO ARMY ABROAD UNLESS U.S. IS ATTACKED

BURMA ROAD PACT AROUSES COMMONS; PEACE DEMAND MET

Japan Reported Ready to Deal With China, but Britons Call 'New Munich' Shameful

QUESTION ON U. S. EVADED

Konoye Forms a Centralized Regime in Tokyo—South Seas Drive Expected

3 British Ports Wrecked By Nazis, Say Dutch Crew

GIBRALTAR DEMAND VOICED BY FRANCO

Chief of State Gives Notice Spain Expects a Part in Post-War Settlement

ARMY OF 2,000,000 A MINIMUM NEED, MARSHALL INSISTS

45 Infantry Divisions and 10 Armored Divisions Are the Objective, General Says

STIMSON HAILS BURKE BILL

Ludicrous for Any One to Oppose Compulsory Service Plan, He Tells Civilian Aides

The Only Ballot

'STAY OUT' PLANK

Goes Slightly Beyond the Recent Pledge of the President

FOR MONROE POLICY

All Material Aid Pledged for Peoples Attacked by Aggressors

AGAIN THE DEMOCRATIC NOMINEE
Franklin Delano Roosevelt

BY 'ACCLAMATION'

Farley, Who Remained in Race, Makes the Vote Unanimous

RIVALS' POLL IS 150

Third-Term Tradition Is Upset—Garner, Tydings Stay to End

PLATFORM MARKED NATION WILL HEAR

Far left: *President Roosevelt examines a Japanese flag captured by a Marine detachment. He declared 7 December 1941, the day of the Japanese attack on Pearl Harbor, 'a day that shall live in infamy.'*

Left: *Roosevelt chats with King Saud of Saudi Arabia on the deck of a US warship. King Saud remained neutral but friendly to the Allies during World War II.*

Below left: *The Big Three meet at Yalta in the Crimea, 4-11 February 1945. President Roosevelt joins Churchill and Stalin in discussing plans for the final phase of the Allies' assault on Germany.*

Right: *FDR with Harry S Truman (vice-president elect) after the election of 1944. Roosevelt died suddenly in April 1945; he is remembered as a strong leader and an extraordinary president.*

Although Roosevelt let the generals and admirals run their operations in the field, he participated in all major strategic decisions. These were usually accomplished through his frequent personal meetings with Prime Minister Winston Churchill of Great Britain and other Allied leaders. Again, as in the Depression, it was Roosevelt's instinctive confidence that kept Americans feeling that they had only to put their shoulders to the wheel to reach their goal.

Roosevelt had run for an unprecedented third term in 1940 on the grounds that only he had the experience to lead the nation into these difficult times. He ran for a yet more controversial fourth term in 1944 on the grounds that it would be unwise to change leaders during a war. His critics said he wanted to become a virtual monarch, but his close associates realized that he might well not make it through those last four years.

Even they did not expect him to die so suddenly, on 12 April 1945, of a massive cerebral hemorrhage. But at least he knew, along with all the Allies, that their long struggle was near an end.

Roosevelt's achievements were many, and he put his stamp on the next 50 years, and very likely for many more, not only with such tangibles as Social Security but by a general expectation that the federal government should become involved in more of the nation's problems. Roosevelt's failings were many: not responding to the plight of the European Jews, allowing Japanese-Americans to be sent to detention camps, underestimating the ambitions of the Russians. But if a president is measured by the difference between the country he started with and the one he left, Franklin Delano Roosevelt's stewardship must be reckoned among the most successful in American history.

Harry S
TRUMAN
1884-1972

Until 1944 probably not one person in a million could have imagined that Harry S Truman would ever be president of the United States, let alone that he would be a great president. He had, to be sure, served in the Senate for 10 years, but his record there, though honorable enough, was hardly brilliant. More to the point, his political influence within the Democratic party was minor, and his following in the national electorate negligable. That he was, in fact, a man of high destiny would have seemed inconceivable to most people, Harry Truman included.

He was born on 8 May 1884 to a farm family in Lamar, Missouri. (His parents gave him no middle name, only the middle initial 'S,' so that both his grandfathers might imagine he had been named after them.) As a boy he was an avid reader, but he failed to receive a hoped-for appointment to West Point because of his poor eyesight. Thus, after graduation from high school, he did not go on to college but worked at a variety of small jobs until taking over the management of the family farm in 1906. He also joined the Missouri National Guard and had attained the rank of Lieutenant by the time the United States entered World War I. He commanded an artillery battery in France, participated in several campaigns and returned home a captain. In 1919 he married his high school sweetheart, Bess Wallace, and opened a men's clothing store. His marriage was entirely successful; his business failed in less than three years.

Left: *Harry S Truman, thirty-third president of the United States, ended World War II and assuaged postwar domestic crises.*

Below: *Truman (far left) in the Truman and Jacobson Haberdashery, a store which served as a gathering place of men of the 129th Field Artillery from November 1919 to 1922.*

Truman decided to try a career in politics and was elected county judge. He served from 1922–34 and gained a reputation for hard work, honesty and fiscal responsibility. In 1934, with the support of 'Big Tom' Prendergast, boss of the Democratic party in Kansas City, Truman was elected to the United States Senate. He proved to be an honest, conscientious senator, but it was not until the onset of World War II that he acquired anything resembling national recognition. In 1941 he was made chairman of the Senate Committee to Investigate the National Defense Program. During the war this committee was to save the country vast sums of money and greatly improve the production of war materiel. It soon came to be known as 'the Truman Committee.'

When Franklin Delano Roosevelt decided to run again in 1944, Democratic leaders were sharply divided over who should be his running mate. Various vice-presidential candidates favored by different wings of the party were unacceptable to the other wings, and Truman was proposed as a sort of innocuous compromise. Roosevelt and Truman won handily, but Truman had

Above: The Chicago Tribune *wrongly announced Thomas E Dewey's victory in the 1948 presidential election.*

Top right: *(l-r) Clement Attlee, Truman and Stalin at their first meeting in 1945.*

Below right: *Truman announces Japan's surrender.*

served only 83 days as vice-president when he was summoned to the White House on 12 April 1945. Told by Mrs Roosevelt that her husband had just died, Truman asked, 'Is there anything I can do for you?' Mrs Roosevelt replied, 'Is there anything *we* can do for *you*? For you are the one in trouble now.'

Although many people initially felt uncomfortable with that 'little man' in the White House, Truman moved decisively in those early months, presiding over the climactic events of World War II and dealing with other Allied leaders. His decision to drop the atomic bombs on Japan, though much criticized in later years, was an action which ended the war, and though he may have yielded too much to Stalin at Potsdam, he was following the course set down by Roosevelt and other Allied leaders.

Left: *President Truman and General MacArthur meet on Wake Island to plan the Korean conflict, 15 October 1950. MacArthur was fired in 1951 when Truman insisted on a policy of limited war in Korea.*

With almost a full term as president ahead of him, Truman continued to act decisively in both domestic and international affairs. He launched the 'Fair Deal,' a series of social programs that were an extension of Roosevelt's New Deal. He set forth the 'Truman Doctrine,' which promised American aid to nations fighting communism. And he supported the Marshall Plan, which gave large sums of money to the war-damaged countries of Europe. Even so, most people felt he had no chance of winning the election of 1948, especially when liberal Democrats nominated a Progressive party candidate and Southern Democrats nominated their own Dixiecrat candidate. Truman himself went to bed on election night thinking he had lost, but he had the pleasure of waking up the winner and displaying a Chicago newspaper with its incautious banner headline, 'Dewey Defeats Truman.'

Truman's second term was dominated by the Korean War, which broke out on 25 June 1950. Truman acted quickly to send American troops, and although the war was formally a United Nations action, it was primarily fought by American forces. As the war dragged on and casualties mounted, Truman came under great pressure, which did not prevent him from removing General Douglas MacArthur as commander of the United Nations forces when he felt that MacArthur was defying his orders. In the end, Truman would leave office with the Korean armistice negotiations at a stalemate.

But Truman could point to other achievements on the international scene. He brought the United States into the North Atlantic Treaty Organization in 1949,

Left: *US Marines with 3.5-inch bazooka and machine gun overlooking a road during the Korean War.*

and in 1950, he persuaded Congress to pass his Point Four Program, which gave millions of dollars to under-developed countries. Truman also advanced other programs that extended American aid to countries for both military and economic improvements. Despite the evident toughness of his foreign policy, some conservatives nevertheless accused Truman of being 'soft on communism' and of somehow 'losing China.' In fact, the methods he used to investigate the presence of communists in the government were questionably harsh. And though Truman was generally supportive of labor, he tried to have the government take over some steel mills to prevent a strike (and was overruled by the Supreme Court in June 1952).

When Truman left office in January 1953 people all over the world had come to realize that the 'little man' was not so little after all. During his long retirement, Truman wrote, lectured and issued opinions from his fittingly named hometown of Independence, Missouri. By his death in 1972, Truman had virtually attained the status of a twentieth-century legend.

Below: *Mr and Mrs Harry Truman in their home in Independence, Missouri, in 1954.*

Dwight David
EISENHOWER
1890-1969

During the 200 years that Americans have been electing their presidents, on several occasions they have turned to wartime heroes to lead them through the immediate postwar years. It does not seem unduly forced to suggest that at least two of these leaders were, in several important ways, remarkably similar. Both were fundamentally conservative yet had little association with any ideological or philosophical position. Both had a barely disguised contempt for conventional party politics. Both displayed few overt signs of ambition yet could be steel-hard in their determination to gain their ends. Above all, both were noted for their ability to command the loyalty and respect of far more assertive and volatile subordinates. Yet for all their similarities, no two men could have been more different in their backgrounds than the patrician George Washington and the humbly born Dwight David Eisenhower.

Eisenhower was born on 14 October 1890 in Denison, Texas, one of seven sons of parents descended from German-Swiss Protestants who had come to America seeking peace and freedom to worship. When Eisenhower was two, his family moved to Abilene, Kansas, where his father worked as a mechanic in a creamery. Although his parents had little formal education, they were determined that their sons would succeed (as indeed they all did); and though their religious beliefs opposed anything to do with the military, they did not stand in young Dwight's way when he was appointed to the United States Military Academy at West Point. He played football there until an injury sidelined him, and he was graduated in 1915, 61st in a class of 164. His first posting was to Fort Sam Houston, near San Antonio, Texas, and there Eisenhower met the woman he soon married, Mamie Geneva Doud. During World War I, Eisenhower did not go overseas but trained stateside tank battalions so well that he was sent on to the prestigious and demanding Command and General Staff School at Fort Leavenworth, Kansas. When he graduated first in his class of 275, he was naturally marked as an officer of promise.

In 1933 Eisenhower was appointed aide to General Douglas MacArthur, Chief of Staff of the United States Army. When MacArthur went to the Philippines in 1935 to help build up that commonwealth's new army, Eisenhower went with him. Back in the United States by 1939, Eisenhower soon earned the nickname 'Alarmist Ike' because he was constantly predicting that America would become involved in the war that was beginning to engulf Europe. After an outstanding performance in the big army maneuvers of the summer of 1941, Eisenhower was promoted to brigadier general. By this time he was highly regarded by General George C Marshall, Chief of Staff of the United States Army, and immediately after Pearl Harbor Marshall assigned Eisenhower to serve in the Army's War Plans Division in Washington. By June 1942, Eisenhower had so impressed certain superiors that he was 'jumped' over 366 senior Army officers to be made commanding general of American

Opposite: *Thirty-fourth president of the United States, Dwight D Eisenhower.*

Left: *Eisenhower with Mamie Geneva Doud, who he married in July 1916.*

Left: *Eisenhower welcoming US reinforcements in France during World War II.*

Below: *Omaha Beach shortly after the first landing, 6 June 1944. Eisenhower was Supreme Commander of the Allied Expeditionary Force.*

Left: *General Eisenhower, Supreme Commander of NATO, confers with President Truman in 1951.*

Below: *Eisenhower in Korea, 1952.*

Right: *'Ike' at the Republican Convention in Chicago, 1952.*

forces in the European Theater of Operations. He immediately set up headquarters in London and directed both the planning and operations that culminated in the invasions of North Africa (November 1942), Sicily (August 1943) and Italy (September 1943).

Then came the grandest operation of all, Overlord, the invasion of Europe along the Normandy coast of France. In December 1943, President Roosevelt, with the approval of Prime Minister Churchill, had appointed Eisenhower Supreme Commander of the Allied Expeditionary Force that would conduct this most massive and complex military operation in the history of mankind. Against great odds he was completely successful, and on 6 June 1944 an astonished world heard the news of the triumphant D Day invasion. From then until the Germans surrendered on 7 May 1945 Eisenhower had to juggle the incredible complexities of military operations across Europe, made harder by the primadonna performances of various American, British and French generals in his theater of operations. But Eisenhower maintained both authority and loyalty, and the major criticism made of him, that he was not the most innovative or daring commander, was probably the very quality that allowed him to hold his team together.

When World War II ended, Eisenhower was as universally admired as Washington had been, and like Washington he claimed he wanted only to retire. But in November 1945, he took over as Chief of Staff of the United States Army and supervised the great demobilization and major reorganization of the nation's armed

forces. Finally, in 1948, Eisenhower did retire to become president of Columbia University, but by December 1950, he was persuaded to return to active duty to serve as the first Supreme Commander of the newly formed North Atlantic Treaty Organization (NATO).

Eisenhower had often been mentioned as a potential presidential candidate, but he had always rejected such overtures. In 1952, however, several influential

Republicans persuaded him to try for that party's nomination. He retired from the army in June, and in July he was nominated on the first ballot. His election was all but guaranteed, and he subsequently took office in January 1953.

One of his campaign promises was 'I shall go to Korea,' to end the war that had been dragging on since June 1950. Eisenhower made the journey shortly after his election, and on 27 July 1953 a truce was finally signed. Other achievements of his first term included the introduction of atomic weapons into the armed forces to replace reliance on large conventional forces, the proposition of the 'Atoms for Peace' initiative, by which all nations would share their knowledge about atomic power in an international atomic energy agency and the formation of the Southeast Asia Treaty Organization

149

Top: *President Eisenhower addresses the United Nations in December 1953. He proposed using the international Atomic Energy Commission to carry out nuclear research in an 'Atoms for Peace' program.*

Above: *President Eisenhower, the first Supreme Allied Commander of Europe, visits Supreme Headquarters Allied Powers Europe near Paris on 3 September 1959.*

Right: *The inauguration ceremony of President Eisenhower and Vice-President Nixon for their second term of office. They won with a very comfortable majority.*

(SEATO). In domestic matters, Eisenhower tried to promote what he called 'modern Republicanism,' striking a balance between federal power and states' rights. The most ambiguous aspect of his first administration was his failure to stop the notorious Senator Joseph McCarthy's red-baiting campaign. Eisenhower hardly supported McCarthyism, but he refused to attack the senator directly.

He easily defeated the Democratic candidate Adlai Stevenson again in 1956, this time with an even larger majority. Among the principal events of his second term were sending federal troops to Little Rock, Arkansas, to enforce the integration of its high school; sending up the first United States space satellite in January 1958, thus launching the United States space program; and pronouncing the 'Eisenhower Doctrine,' which pledged United States military aid to any Middle Eastern nation asking for help against communist aggression. Much of

Above: *Eisenhower signs the Civil Rights Act of 1957, establishing the Civil Rights Commission and providing penalties for violation of the voting rights of any US citizen.*

Above right: *Soviet premier Nikita S Khrushchev is welcomed to the United States by President Eisenhower at Andrews Air Force Base on 15 September 1959.*

Right: *French President de Gaulle salutes before Eisenhower's coffin. People throughout the world mourned his death.*

Eisenhower's energies throughout his eight years as president were focused on the deteriorating relations with Russia and the communist world. There was the so-called U-2 incident, for example, when a United States spy plane, a U-2, was shot down over Russia, leading the Soviet leader, Nikita Khrushchev, to cancel a planned summit meeting with Eisenhower; and there was the diplomatic break with Cuba in January 1961 after Fidel Castro seized American property in Cuba and accused the United States of 'counter-revolutionary activities.'

When Eisenhower left office in 1960, Congress restored his rank of General of the Army, but he never returned to active service and retired to his farm in Gettysburg, Pennsylvania. His health declined, but not his standing in the hearts of many Americans and people throughout the world, all of whom mourned his death on 28 March 1969. Although during his presidency he was criticized by some for not having taken stronger stands on a variety of pressing social issues, subsequent historians have tended to rate his administrations highly. His style of leadership – relaxed, avuncular, fundamentally strong – gave just the kind of assurance needed by a nation that was all too rapidly coming to understand the somber implications of living in the age of the Cold War and the Atom.

John Fitzgerald
KENNEDY
1917-1963

It is common for presidents to be criticized while in office and only later to be lauded for their accomplishments and virtues. The historical fate of John F Kennedy has been rather the opposite. He was exceptionally popular during his time in office and after his martyrdom, but his 'Camelot' era eventually became tarnished by the steady accumulation of hindsight. Regardless of what he finally accomplished, however, there is no question as to the vitality and sense of promise he brought to the presidency.

Kennedy was born to a prominent Massachusetts Irish Catholic family in Brookline on 29 May 1917 and was brought up in a stimulating and highly competitive atmosphere. Patriarch Joseph Kennedy was a ruthlessly ambitious politician who eventually became ambassador to Great Britain. He seemed determined that at least one of his children would be a president.

After being graduated from Harvard in 1940, John Kennedy published his senior thesis as *Why England Slept*; it became a best seller. He joined the Navy during World War II and was captain of a torpedo boat that was sunk by the Japanese in 1943. Kennedy saved his crew and gained decorations and a hero's reputation. In that action he also injured his back, resulting in a life of steady pain that he bore stoically.

Elected to the United States House of Representatives as a Democrat in 1947, Kennedy went on to take the Senate seat of Massachusetts Republican stalwart Henry Cabot Lodge in 1952. While recovering from a back operation in 1954, Kennedy wrote *Profiles in Courage*, a book that won a Pulitzer Prize in 1956. In that year, he made a bid for the vice-presidency. Failing that, he began to prepare for the next convention. In 1960, he first defeated Democrat Lyndon Johnson for the

Below: *The Kennedy family in the 1930s. John F Kennedy is in the center.*

Right: *John F Kennedy became the thirty-fifth president of the United States in 1960.*

Left: *The young Kennedy as an officer in the Pacific during World War II.*

Below left: *Kennedy with his wife Jacqueline at their wedding in 1953. Kennedy was senator of Massachusetts at the time.*

Right: *President Kennedy greets Premier Khrushchev at the US Embassy in Vienna, 3 June 1961.*

nomination (Johnson took the vice-presidential spot) and then narrowly beat Richard Nixon in the election. At 43, Kennedy was the youngest man ever elected to the presidency, and the only Catholic. His youthful wife, Jacqueline, may have been the most glamorous of First Ladies.

In his inaugural address, Kennedy set the upbeat tone of his administration with his ringing peroration, 'Ask not what your country can do for you; ask what you can do for your country.' (The phrase had first been used by Warren G Harding.) Soon thereafter came a near disaster. Kennedy approved an invasion of Cuba's Bay of Pigs in April 1961 by exiles from that communist island (this had been planned in the Eisenhower era). When the invasion proved a fiasco, Kennedy gamely shouldered the blame, and his popularity was not greatly affected.

In his first months in office, Kennedy proclaimed a 'New Frontier' and sent a flood of progressive legislation to Congress. This included medical care for the aged, federal aid to education, a stepped-up space program and several civil rights proposals. Over the next two years, however, Kennedy was able to get few of his measures through Congress. Only after his death did many of these ideas come to fruition under Lyndon Johnson. More successful in his foreign policy initiatives, Kennedy oversaw the creation of the Alliance for Progress with Latin America and the Peace Corps, which sent young Americans to work in developing countries.

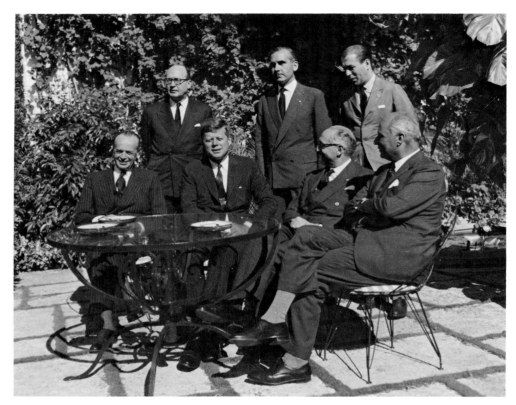

Left: *JFK meets with Cuban exile leaders in Miami, 27 December 1962.*

Below left: *Missile equipment at the Mariel Port Facility in Cuba, 4 November 1962. Kennedy's clever handling of the Cuban Missile Crisis led to the Nuclear Test Ban Treaty of 1963 and better communications between Moscow and Washington.*

Right: *Kennedy's coffin passes before his widow Jacqueline and his brothers Edward (left) and Robert (right). The assassination of 22 November 1963 shocked the world; Kennedy's charisma and youth had symbolized a bright future for America in the hopeful days of the early 1960s.*

His great crisis came in October 1962 when it was discovered that Russia was sending missiles to Castro's Cuba. Kennedy proclaimed a blockade on weapons shipments to Cuba and demanded that the missile bases be dismantled. While the world held its breath (Kennedy himself calculated a one in two chance of avoiding nuclear war), Russia blustered and then backed off. Having bested the Russians without humiliating them, Kennedy pressed for better relations, and that led, in August 1963, to the signing of a landmark treaty with Russia and Britain ending atmospheric testing of nuclear weapons.

With these victories on his record, his response to growing turmoil in Vietnam still undecided, his New Frontier programs still pending in Congress and the nation experiencing unprecedented prosperity, Kennedy headed for Texas on a speechmaking tour. On 22 November 1963, a stunned world learned of his assassination in Dallas by Lee Harvey Oswald, evidently disturbed but with unknown motives. Of the many eulogies that followed, perhaps British Prime Minister Harold MacMillan sounded the truest note: 'He seemed, in his own person, to embody all the hopes and aspirations of this new world that is struggling to emerge.' Despite Kennedy's lack of substantial accomplishment while in office, and despite subsequent revelations about some unseemly aspects of his private life, MacMillan's judgment of him still obtains.

Lyndon Baines
JOHNSON
1908-1973

Whatever Lyndon Johnson did throughout his long career in politics, he did it big, with the brash and expansive spirit of the Texas land that bred him. He made a big name for himself, created a big surge forward in justice for the disadvantaged and finally started a big war that in the end destroyed both much that he had labored for and the great name in history that he had coveted.

Johnson was born in the town where he died, Stonewall, Texas, on 27 August 1908. During the 1930s, he taught school for a couple of years and then went to work for the New Deal and the Democrats in Texas. That experience and the contacts he made took him to the United States House of Representatives in 1937.

Johnson was a relatively lackluster figure in the House, but his career was assisted by fellow Texan Sam Rayburn, later to become Speaker of the House. By 1948 Johnson felt strong enough to run for the Senate and was elected by a margin of 87 votes out of one million cast. Once in the Senate, he rose quickly, showing a talent both for making deals and for twisting arms when necessary. By 1953 he was minority leader and two years later majority leader; despite a heart attack that year, he had cemented his position as one of the strongest and ablest men on Capitol Hill. The thrust of his efforts then and later was surprising for a Texan reputed to be only moderately liberal: Johnson became a primary initiator of some of the most progressive social legislation in American history. Most notably, he led the fight for the landmark civil rights acts of 1957 and 1960, and was in the forefront of action on social welfare programs. His partner in these triumphs was his protégé, Hubert Humphrey.

Less surprisingly, Johnson set his sights on the presidency, and in 1960 he made his move. But the Democratic Convention of that year was attracted to a man every bit as wily as Lyndon Johnson – John F Kennedy. In an effort to unify the party, the victorious

Below: *Lyndon B Johnson being sworn in as president aboard Air Force 1 on 22 November 1963.*

Right: *Lyndon B Johnson, thirty-sixth president of the United States.*

Opposite: *Johnson addressing the Senate and other US leaders as he signs the Civil Rights Bill at the White House on 2 July 1964. The bill outlawed discrimination in all public places and was the most far-reaching of its kind since the Reconstruction.*

Above: *President Johnson meets Vietnam's foreign minister Pham Huy Quat on 9 June 1964.*

Left: *This 1964 cartoon showing Johnson as a Texas cowboy depicts his vigorous domestic policy and cautious foreign policy.*

Kennedy offered Johnson the vice-presidential slot. Though he did not relish the prospect, he was a loyal party man and accepted, settling without complaint into the near-anonymity of the vice-presidency. Then, a thousand days later, he found himself taking the oath of office beside a blood-spattered Jacqueline Kennedy.

Like a Texas cowboy he stormed into the presidency with guns ablaze, shaking the whole of Washington with the force of his personality. He was awkward, crude, thin-skinned, overly concerned with matters of personal loyalty and unforgiving of hostile critics. At the same time, he was a consummate politician whose primary goal and intended memorial in history was the building of a more fair and open America, a vision that he called the Great Society. Moreover, he had a Democratically-controlled Congress filled with colleagues who owed him loyalty and favors. Skillfully manipulating Congressional support, he declared war on poverty and pushed through an astonishingly wide-ranging series of bills and programs: Medicare, expanded aid to education and a collection of antipoverty programs. In addition he sponsored the most extensive civil rights program since the Civil War, including open housing and the epochal 1965 Voting Rights Act.

These efforts (some of them begun under Kennedy, to be sure) carried into Johnson's second term. He won by a landslide over Republican Barry Goldwater in November 1964, bringing with him as vice-president his old partner Hubert Humphrey. Yet even before that moment of triumph, Johnson's career had begun to show the first signs of being blighted by the increasingly sinister turn of events in Vietnam. In August 1964, after an alleged attack on American patrol boats in the waters off Vietnam, Johnson asked for and received from Congress the Gulf of Tonkin Resolution. This gave him a virtual free hand to wage war in Vietnam, and Johnson used that power far beyond what anyone expected.

He believed that communism posed the same kind of threat to the world that Germany did before World

Top: *LBJ meeting with the attorney general and secretary of defense on the Detroit riots, 24 July 1967.*

Above: *Johnson decorates a young soldier in Vietnam, 23 December 1967. He was criticized for escalating the war in Vietnam without popular support.*

Above right: *Johnson was very proud of his LBJ Ranch in Texas.*

War II, and he was convinced that it was America's task to nip this menace in the bud. He ordered massive bombing of North Vietnam, and over the next four years he escalated American troop commitments until there were nearly half a million men fighting and dying in the forests and rice paddies of that small Asian country. Just as the French had learned in blood and defeat a decade earlier, the United States slowly began to realize that its efforts were going nowhere.

As the war blundered on, anti-war sentiment at home became so intense that the American social fabric itself seemed in danger of unravelling. During those years, as his Great Society programs were drained by the cost of war, Johnson increasingly barricaded himself from criticism, but by 1967 he found he could not ignore the defectors within his own administration, among them Secretary of Defense Robert MacNamara and his replacement Clark Clifford.

Johnson saw the handwriting on the wall when, in the first presidential primary of 1968, he only narrowly defeated Eugene McCarthy, whose sole issue was to end the war. On 31 March Johnson stunned the nation by announcing that he would not run for re-election. As a last show of strength he helped his old friend Humphrey gain the nomination, but he may have ruined Humphrey's chances by insisting on his loyalty and not allowing him to distance himself from the war. The result was victory for Richard Nixon and the Republicans. Exhausted, ill and disappointed, Johnson retired to his ranch. He died there on 22 January 1973.

Richard Milhous
NIXON
1913-1994

Having risen to prominence by the dubious but effective means of 'red-baiting', Richard Nixon pursued his career in public life with a series of actions that were sometimes brilliant, sometimes astonishingly petty and self-defeating. His eventual downfall produced a national trauma of massive proportions.

Born in Yorba Linda, California, on 9 January 1913, Nixon gained a law degree from Duke University in 1937. After Navy service he returned to California and in 1946 ran for the United States House of Representatives. Showing the campaign style he would use for some time, he vaguely implied that his opponent was communist-supported. Thereby winning the election, he rocketed to fame in the House as a member of the Un-American Activities Committee, especially with his vigorous prosecution of the spy case against Alger Hiss. Thus it was as a national figure that Nixon ran for the Senate in 1950. Nixon branded his opponent, Helen Gahagan Douglas, the 'Pink Lady.' Again the tactic worked, and Nixon continued his ascent.

In 1952 the young senator became Eisenhower's running mate, but only by the skin of his teeth. Charged with improper use of campaign funds in his Senate race,

Far left: *Richard Nixon was the thirty-seventh president of the United States. His success in foreign policy was overshadowed by the Watergate scandal of 1972.*

Left: *The 'Kitchen Debate' in Moscow, 1959, between Premier Nikita Khrushchev and Vice-President Richard Nixon.*

Above: *After his service as a naval officer in the South Pacific during World War II, Nixon returned to Whittier, California, to practice law with the firm of Bewley, Knoop and Nixon.*

Nixon appeared on national television with a dramatic self-defense (that came to be known as the 'Checkers' speech, after the family dog). Though maudlin, theatrical and somewhat beside the point, the speech was well received by the voters, and Nixon remained on the Eisenhower team that swept into office in 1952.

As vice-president, Nixon revealed unsuspected strengths. Conservative though he was, he was nonetheless an internationalist in outlook, and his civil rights record was surprisingly moderate. As a representative of the administration, he was a dutiful and strong advocate, whether riding out anti-American riots in Venezuela or standing up to Khrushchev in Moscow. In 1960 this more moderate and mature 'new Nixon' came before the public as the Republican presidential contender.

But the election went to Kennedy, and it seemed that Nixon's hopes for the presidency had faded. The apparent last straw came in 1962, when he lost a race for governor of California and, in an embarrassing outburst, snarled at the press, 'You won't have Dick Nixon to kick around anymore.' As it turned out, they would have that chance for years to come.

Above: *American involvement in Vietnam became more and more unpopular during Nixon's presidency. Students held protests against the war, and clashes with the police sometimes provoked violent confrontations.*

Right: *Nixon and his wife Pat receiving a ticker-tape welcome in New York City.*

Below: *A youth rally in Washington DC.*

Left: *President Nixon talks with members of the 1st Infantry Division during his 1969 tour of Vietnam.*

Below: *Nixon was president when Neil Armstrong first set foot on the moon, 21 July 1969.*

Right: *Chairman Mao Tse-Tung and President Nixon at Mao's home in China, 22 February 1972. Nixon has to his credit the re-opening of negotiations with China as well as the establishment of détente with the Soviet Union.*

Below right: *President Nixon with Secretary of State Dr Henry Kissinger.*

By 1968 Nixon had so rebuilt his political career as again to become the Republican presidential nominee. His opponent, Hubert Humphrey, was tainted by his past support of the Vietnam War. Promising a 'secret plan to end the war,' Nixon and running mate Spiro Agnew won the election. Nixon came to the White House with much of his past popularity intact, but at the same time there were nagging questions about his integrity that long ago had earned him the nickname 'Tricky Dick.' All in all, he was an enigma, his personality and basic values a closed book. Years before, Adlai Stevenson had called him a 'plausible young man of flexible convictions.'

Nixon initiated a moderately conservative program: cuts in government spending, anticrime legislation, creation of a new antiballistic missile system and so on. Claiming he was winding down the war, he pursued a policy called 'Vietnamization.' In practice, that meant gradual American troop withdrawals combined with enormously stepped-up bombing. But undoubtedly his most surprising actions were his gestures of peace to China and the Soviet Union. With Russia he pursued a policy of détente and negotiated a significant arms reduction treaty. Similarly, he announced American recognition of communist China and made an unprecedented visit there in 1972.

Meanwhile the country was undergoing some of the worst turmoil of its history: many college campuses were in revolt, and one such anti-war demonstration led to the fatal shooting of four students at Kent State University in 1970. Amid this tumult, Nixon struck back forcefully at opponents of all stripes, authorizing illegal wiretaps, break-ins and harassment of political enemies. But the full extent and nature of these activities would not become public until much later.

Nixon swamped antiwar Democrat George McGovern in the 1972 election. Soon thereafter the negotiations for a ceasefire and settlement in Vietnam were concluded, and America's longest war was over. Hardly noticed amid these great events was the ongoing investigation of a puzzling event that had occurred in June 1972: the burgling of the Democratic party headquarters in Washington's Watergate Hotel. Within the next 18 months the instigation of the Watergate burglary had been traced to the White House, vice-

president Agnew had conceded charges of corruption and resigned (to be replaced by Gerald Ford), many of Nixon's Cabinet members and advisors faced criminal charges and prison, Nixon himself had been assessed nearly a half million dollars in improper tax deductions and the discovery of potentially incriminating secret tapes of White House conversations had effectively undone the Nixon presidency. Finally, in the face of certain impeachment, in August 1974 Nixon became the first president to resign. One month later, President Gerald Ford gave Nixon a full pardon. Nixon subsequently retired from the political stage, but in his final years he regained something of his reputation as an astute observer of contemporary affairs.

Above: *The historic television broadcast of Nixon's resignation.*

Left: *Threatened with impeachment for unwarranted extensions of executive powers during the Watergate affair, Nixon announced his resignation on 9 August 1974.*

Right: *Nixon boarding his helicopter after his resignation. The double 'peace sign' was his trademark.*

Gerald Rudolph
FORD
1913-

Gerald Ford was the first man to gain both the vice-presidency and the presidency having been elected to neither office. Certainly he was the first to ascend on the resignation of a president, and the overriding task of his administration was to restore confidence in an executive branch compromised by the scandals of the Nixon era.

Ford was born in Omaha, Nebraska, on 14 July 1913 and played on championship football teams at the University of Michigan. From college he went to Yale, where he coached sports and gained a law degree. After Navy service during World War II he practiced law in Michigan and was elected to Congress in 1948. For some 15 years the affable and low-keyed Ford was a dutiful Republican stalwart in the House. In 1965 he emerged into the limelight as House minority leader, at which post he remained until 1973.

That year, Richard Nixon appointed Ford his vice-president. The previous holder of the job, Spiro Agnew, had resigned in the face of criminal charges. Unlike many previous Nixon appointees, Ford was loyal and manifestly honest. In August 1974 the rising tide of Watergate overwhelmed Nixon, who resigned rather than face impeachment. Gerald Ford thus became the 38th president.

Left: *Gerald R Ford became the thirty-eighth president of the United States upon Nixon's resignation.*

Below: *Ford played football at the University of Michigan. This photo is from 1934.*

Left: *President Ford and his wife Betty (both in center) meet King Hussein of Jordan and his wife in 1976.*

Below: *Ford addresses the nation following the pardon of ex-president Nixon, 8 September 1974.*

Top: *Secretary of State Henry Kissinger showing a map of Cambodia to Congressional leaders as they are briefed on the* Mayaguez *incident, 22 May 1975. Ford (on left) successfully handled the affair, in which a US cargo ship was seized by Cambodia's Khmer Rouge government.*

Above: *Ford addresses a Joint Session of Congress, asking for aid for Vietnam and Cambodia of some $722 million. On 30 April 1975 the last US troops were evacuated from Vietnam as the Saigon government surrendered to the Communists.*

A month later, Ford gave Nixon full pardon from criminal prosecution. That action, perhaps stemming from Ford's party loyalty and personal compassion, was more courageous than politic, and the reaction of the country to the pardon was largely negative. He had other problems as well, most notably a serious recession combined with inflation and high unemployment.

In the latter part of his presidency these economic woes began to recede somewhat, and Ford won a measure of acclaim for his handling of the *Mayaguez* incident, when he took military action to free an American ship seized by Cambodia. Continuing Nixon's policy of détente with Russia, Ford met with Soviet leader Leonid Brezhnev; and when South Vietnam collapsed in 1975, Ford evacuated the remaining Americans and some refugees with a minimum of fuss.

Yet Ford had still not secured the nation's full approval. In 1976 he had a tough fight, gaining the Republican nomination over rival Ronald Reagan, but having won that battle, he lost the election to Jimmy Carter, who had campaigned on promises not to pursue politics as usual; after Watergate, that was what the nation wanted to hear. Ford conceded defeat in a tearful and moving television appearance. He retired to write and lecture. His tenure as president had been short: his accomplishment – to restore public trust in the presidency – had not been inconsiderable.

James Earl (Jimmy)
CARTER
1924-

The fact that Jimmy Carter insisted on being called by his boyhood nickname was typical of his new approach to the presidency: informal, open and personal. In the wake of the Watergate nightmare, Carter's platform promised a government of truth, compassion and liberal activism. But once he was in office, the policies of this relative newcomer to politics were largely to be frustrated.

He was born in the country town of Plains, Georgia, on 1 October 1924. A graduate of the United States Naval Academy, he briefly pursued a Navy career and then returned to Plains to develop a successful peanut-farming business. His liberal social ideals, especially in racial matters, took him into politics as a Democrat. In 1962 he was elected to the first of two terms in the Georgia senate. After an unsuccessful bid for the governorship in 1970, he gained that office in the next election. During his one term (by law he could not succeed himself) he reorganized the state government, appointed many blacks to office and pushed for extensive environmental legislation. In all these efforts he found only partial success, and his troubles in managing the legislature prefigured similar problems in Washington.

After leaving the governorship, Carter, to everyone's astonishment, set his sights on the presidency. With the help of a few associates he gradually made his name known to the nation. Carter astutely played on the nation's post-Watergate malaise. His earnest promises of honesty and open government gave his candidacy a meteoric rise, which ended in the defeat of Gerald Ford in 1976. Though his winning margin was small, Carter had risen from obscurity to unseat an incumbent in less than one year.

Carter immediately unleashed a flood of activity. He gave full pardon to Vietnam draft evaders, created a Cabinet-level energy post, submitted bills to reorganize the government, proclaimed human rights a major foreign policy objective, pushed successfully for returning the Panama Canal to Panama, inaugurated full diplomatic relations with mainland China and oversaw the Salt II treaty with Moscow. Yet his inexperience and lack of a power base in Washington caused many of his initiatives to founder. Neither his energy program nor the Salt II treaty could be got past Congress. Meanwhile inflation and unemployment soared, and the nation began to suspect that Carter had no power to control them.

His greatest moment came in 1978, when Carter singlehandedly did what had seemed impossible. He persuaded Egyptian President Anwar Sadat and Israeli leader Menachem Begin to make peace by signing the

Above: *Democrat Carter's relaxed, informal style impressed many Americans who were impatient with the Republicans.*

Right: *Thirty-ninth president of the United States James Earl (Jimmy) Carter was the first president from the Deep South since 1848.*

Left: *Carter arranged the 1978 Camp David meeting between Egyptian President Anwar Sadat (left) and Israeli Prime Minister Menachem Begin (right).*

Below: *Carter attends services for the Iranian-held hostages, 15 November 1979. Also shown are Vice-President Walter Mondale and Secretary of State Cyrus Vance. The hostage crisis cast a shadow over Carter's presidency.*

Camp David accords. But that could not arrest the decline of his popularity. As the nation increasingly questioned Carter's overall competence and control, the final disaster erupted, in November 1979, when Shiite radicals took American embassy employees hostage in Iran. As months went by Americans saw a president powerless in the face of Iranian effrontery. Almost simultaneously, the Soviet Union invaded Afghanistan, an action that infuriated the president, who felt personally betrayed by the Soviet leadership, and relations between the superpowers abruptly worsened. These crises, combined with the declining economic situation, prepared Carters' decisive defeat by Ronald Reagan in 1980. In retirement, Carter gained a new respect for his continual efforts promoting peace, fair elections, and humanitarian projects.

Below left: *President Carter and Chinese Vice-President Bo Yibo sign trade agreements at the White House, 25 September 1980.*

Ronald Wilson
REAGAN
1911-2004

Left: *Ronald Reagan, fortieth president of the United States.*

Above: *Reagan was a movie actor before he became involved in politics; he usually played the nice guy. He is shown here in one of his former Western film roles.*

During the 1950s, the nation watched actor Ronald Reagan on television as he intoned in his firm and reassuring voice: 'At General Electric, progress is our most important product.' More than two decades later, the nation watched him on television saying that massive weapons buildups were the road to peace. He proved equally convincing in both roles, the second of which was as president.

Reagan was born in Tampico, Illinois, in February 1911. While a young radio announcer he was discovered by a Hollywood agent in 1937 and went on to become as he later put it, 'king of the Bs' [second-string films]. He appeared in over 50 movies, some of which, such as *King's Row*, won critical praise.

Reagan spent most of the 1940s as a New Deal Democrat. In 1947 he became president of the Screen Actors Guild, thus becoming the only United States president to have headed a labor union. By 1950 his politics had become more conservative, and his concern about communist infiltration in Hollywood led to a brief period when he reported on the activities of fellow actors to the FBI. Divorced from actress Jane Wyman, Reagan married another actress, Nancy Davis, in 1952. This union would prove to be happy and enduring.

Having switched to the Republican Party, Reagan made a 1964 television speech in support of Barry Goldwater for the presidency. A group of businessmen, liking what they saw, recruited him to run for governor of California. Lambasting campus radicals and welfare cheaters, Reagan won the governorship in 1966 by an unprecedented margin. In office, he cut taxes by four million dollars and worked to reduce government spending (though, in fact, the state budget more than doubled during his tenure). He

Left: *Reagan poses with the members of the United States Supreme Court. To his left is Chief Justice Warren E. Burger. Associate Justice Thurgood Marshall (second from left) was the first black to serve on the court; Associate Justice Sandra Day O'Connor (to the right of the president) was the court's first woman, appointed by Reagan in 1981.*

Left: *Assassination attempt: President Reagan waves to onlookers a split second before the would-be assassin fired his pistol, 30 March 1981.*

Below: *President Reagan greets Prime Minister Menachem Begin of Israel on his arrival at the White House, September 1981. They discussed Middle East problems and the sale of AWAC planes to the Arabs.*

Opposite: *US troops in Beirut, Lebanon, after the US embassy was bombed.*

also cut back significantly on welfare spending. In the process, he endeared himself to conservatives around the country, which led to his efforts to gain the Republican presidential nomination in 1968 and again in 1976, when he nearly took the nomination from Gerald Ford.

By 1980 the country, suffering from inflation, high unemployment and the Iranian hostage crisis, had grown weary of President Carter's chilly style and apparent ineptitude, and the affable, witty and photogenic Reagan was swept into office on a conservative tidal wave. He at once set about honoring his promise to remake the prevailing American government.

That meant lower spending, lower taxes, less regulation and a rollback of government activism in the areas of civil rights, environmental policy and social welfare. As part of what was dubbed 'Reagonomics,' he made deep cuts in personal and business taxes and in general propounded the view that increased productivity, rather than social programs, would be most beneficial to the nation as a whole. His economic advisors had impressive credentials, but many of their theories proved to be, infact, impracticable.

His refusal to commit the Federal government to legalization of abortion alienated many advocates of women's rights, but he did take a mildly controversial step in appointing the first woman to the Supreme Court—Associate Justice Sandra Day O'Connor.

During his first term the results of his actions were mixed. Inflation indeed plummeted and unemployment lowered. The middle class and the rich found themselves with more money than they had had in some time, and in general the economy seemed robust and healthy. On the other hand, the reduction in taxes was not replaced by new revenue, and deficit spending shot up ominously toward the $200-billion mark. Nor did the economic improvement immediately bring the hoped-for benefits to the poor: the number of people living below the poverty level actually increased to some degree.

In the matter of relations between the superpowers Reagan perpetuated the hard line that his predecessor, Jimmy Carter, had adopted after the Soviet invasion of Afghanistan in late 1979. Unlike Carter, Reagan backed up his harsh words about Soviet policies by initiating the largest peacetime military buildup in American history. Yet the ways in which he employed this gathering military power were relatively restrained: a failed attempt at peacekeeping in civil-war-torn Lebanon, the overthrow of a pro-Cuban regime on the tiny Caribbean island of Grenada and a certain amount of sabre-rattling directed at Marxist Nicaragua (to whose anti-government rebel forces he supplied aid) and at belligerently anti-American Libya. One of his most controversial policies was the Strategic Defense Initiative (promptly dubbed 'Star Wars' by the press)—a large-scale research program aimed at finding ways to intercept incoming enemy missiles in space.

If there were questions about Reagan's policies, there could be none about his personal popularity: in the 1984 national election he defeated Democrat Walter Mondale by winning more electoral votes than any presidential candidate in history. Soon thereafter he began a series of summit meetings with new Soviet President Mikhail Gorbachev that culminated in 1987's epochal INF Treaty banning US and Soviet intermediate-range nuclear missiles from Europe. On the home front, meanwhile, matters were going less well. The Democrats had won control of both houses of Congress in 1986, and by 1987 they were gleefully holding hearings on a jucy scandal, the 'Iran-Contra Affair,' in which top administration aides, who hoped to free US hostages in the Middle East, had covertly sold arms to Iran and then had used the proceeds illegally to fund anti-government rebels in Nicaragua.

Though a majority of voters seemed to believe Reagan when he said he knew nothing of this operation, at the least his management abilities came into question, and his popularity dipped – only to rebound again in the last year of his second term. Indeed, the abiding affection in which he was held by the American people even in the face of controversy or disappointment was one of the great hallmarks of the Reagan presidency. Reagan died on 5 June 2004, at the age of 93, after a long battle with Alzheimer's disease.

George
BUSH
1924–

On 8 November 1988 George Herbert Walker Bush became the first serving vice-president since Martin Van Buren to be elected directly to the presidency of the United States. It was an event that not many people would have predicted a year earlier. According to conventional wisdom then, 1988 was supposed to be a Democratic year. True, President Reagan's personal popularity still remained high, but, it was said, the cumulative effect of the Iran-Contra scandal, the runaway budget and trade deficits and the unimpressive gains made in the war on poverty, drugs and environmental pollution had fatally eroded public faith in Reagan's—and by extension, the Republican Party's—policies. Yet Vice-President Bush, with a little help from a lackluster Democratic campaign, proved that once again conventional wisdom was wrong.

Bush is a New Englander who made his fortune and started his political career in Texas. He was born into an old and prominent Connecticut family (his father was a US Senator) on 12 June 1924. After graduation from Phillips Andover Academy (1942) he joined the US Navy. For his service as a World War II carrier pilot, he was awarded the Distinguished Flying Cross and three Air Medals. In 1945 he married Barbara Pierce, daughter of the publisher of *McCalls Magazine*, and then returned to school to complete his education. Not long after Bush received his AB in economics from Yale in 1948, he and his bride moved south to Texas, where Bush soon became involved in the booming oil business. By the early 1950s he had become a co-founder of the highly successful Zapata Petroleum Co., and he subsequently served as president, and later chairman, of Zapata's Off Shore Company in Houston.

Left: *George Bush, Ronald Reagan's political heir, was elected the 41st US president in 1988.*

Below: *In the hard-fought 1988 campaign the Bushes pause to address a crowd at Disneyland.*

Left: *Bush as he was in 1972, when he served as the US ambassador to the United Nations.*

Right: *US President George Bush and his top advisors receive a briefing on the US military response to the Iraqi invasion of Kuwait at the Pentagon in 1990. Seen here are (left to right) General H Norman Schwarzkopf, US Army, Commander-in-Chief; Secretary of Defense Dick Cheney; and President Bush.*

Below: *Bush greets future voters during his presidential campaign.*

By the 1960s his interests were shifting to politics. He began as chairman of his local county Republican Party organization, then unsuccessfully ran for the US Senate in 1964; in 1966 and 1968 he was elected to the US House of Representatives. (By this time he had sold his interests in the oil business.) During the Nixon and Ford administrations he took on a series of appointments: ambassador to the United Nations, special envoy to China, and directorship of the CIA. In 1980, after an unsuccessful bid for the Republican presidential nomination, he accepted Ronald Reagan's offer of the vice-presidential slot. Their ticket won by a landslide, as it did again in 1984.

When Bush ran for the presidency in 1988, most people were unsure of just what kind of a leader he would make. His first major test came in December 1989 when General Manuel Noriega, the president of Panama wanted by the US courts as a drug trafficker, allowed his forces to challenge US personnel in Panama, killing one US officer. Bush ordered an invasion that had effectively taken over Panama within 48 hours. On 3 January 1990,

Noriega was captured and flown to the United States for trial. Although criticized by many for this action, Bush had demonstrated his decisiveness. But his greatest test came when Iraq invaded Kuwait in August 1990: Bush responded firmly, organized a massive international force and, again despite his critics, presided over the successful war in the Persian Gulf.

Some would argue, however, that Bush's most significant achievement came less from such actions than from his non-activity as the USSR and its 'empire' in Eastern Europe was crumbling during his term: Bush neither interfered nor exploited the events and in 1990 he could declare the end of the Cold War.

Unfortunately, this same tendency toward caution was Bush's undoing when it came to domestic affairs. As the economy slipped into a recession and unemployment rose, Bush seemed unwilling to take steps to remedy the situation. His popularity following the Gulf War collapsed, and in a surprising upset he lost the election to Bill Clinton in 1992. Bush retired to private life, apparently content to enjoy life with his family.

William Jefferson (Bill)
CLINTON
1946–

When Bill Clinton first came to the attention of most Americans, it was not in the most favorable light: he was roundly, if somewhat humorously, criticized for his painfully lengthy nominating speech of Michael Dukakis at the 1988 Democratic Convention. Few would have anticipated that four years later Clinton would be back making his own acceptance speech at a Democratic convention.

Clinton was born William Jefferson Blythe IV in Hope, Arkansas, on August 19, 1946. His father had died in a traffic accident two months earlier, and when his mother remarried four years later, the boy was given his stepfather's surname, Clinton. Even as a high school student he showed an avid interest in politics, and he went to Georgetown University in Washington, DC, where he majored in international relations. His two years (1968-70) as a Rhodes Scholar at Oxford University, England, would later become controversial, as this was during the thick of the Vietnam War and he appeared to have exploited his student status to avoid military

service. He returned to attend Yale Law School, where he met fellow student Hillary Rodham; he graduated in 1973 and they were married in 1975. He returned to Arkansas to teach law at the university's law school; in 1976, a committed Democrat, he won election as its attorney general. He became governor (1979-81) and, failing to win re-election, he went back to basics and regained the governorship in 1982; he was re-elected three more times, then stepped aside to run for president. Regarded as a long shot at the outset, he defeated George Bush in November 1992, although because of the strong showing by H Ross Perot, Clinton gained the office with only 43 percent of the popular vote.

Left: *William Jefferson (Bill) Clinton, the 42nd president of the United States, was elected in 1992 and re-elected in 1996.*

Below: *Democratic presidential candidate Bill Clinton shakes hands with students in Connecticut during a stop on the campaign trail in 1992.*

Left: *Bill Clinton with wife Hillary and vice-presidential candidate Al Gore with wife Tipper greet supporters at a rally in Chicago in 1992.*

Right: *US President Bill Clinton and China's President Jiang Zemin shake hands at a joint press conference at the White House in October 1997.*

Below: *President Clinton stands amongst American troops in Tuzla during an executive visit to Bosnia in 1996.*

Assuming the presidency in January 1993, Clinton soon conducted himself in a way that would be repeated, to some criticism, during his years in office: he seemed to be taking a bold stand–in this first instance, allowing homosexuals in the military–and then backed away from his position. He would do this on several occasions: nominating individuals to high posts but withdrawing when controversy arose, insisting on the primacy of human rights and then downplaying this when it came to dealings with China, speaking out for environmental preservation but backing away from a strong stand when it came to protests from business interests, opposing cutbacks for the poor but signing a drastic welfare reform bill. For these and other similar actions, Clinton came to gain a reputation for being something of a 'waffler,' a compromiser.

But the fact was that Clinton found himself in an exceptionally difficult position: after the Congressional elections of 1994, he was forced to conduct his presidency confronted by a Republican-controlled Congress. This greatly limited his ability to take direct action. As the majority party, the Republicans held the positions of power including the committee chairs, and many of these people were blatantly opposed to Clinton, both ideologically and personally.

It was widely observed, in fact, that seldom in recent times had a president been subjected to so much personal venom and attacks. In part this came about because of the emergence of a more conservative and ideological Republican membership in Congress. But in part it was due to Clinton's own behavior. He was linked to compromising situations with women outside his marriage.

Meanwhile, Hillary Rodham Clinton, a distinguished lawyer in her own right, seemed at the outset to be taking a stronger role in governmental affairs than some Americans thought was appropriate. Then there was the Whitewater Affair: a complex series of questionable real estate and bank deals which had occurred in Arkansas while Clinton was governor. Year after year, Republican-dominated hearings attempted to link both Clintons to illegal actions, and although no formal charges were ever brought against them, undoubtedly the president emerged somewhat tarnished.

None of this, however, proved sufficient to keep Clinton from winning re-election in 1996, this time defeating Robert Dole quite handily (although with only 49 percent of the popular vote). In part this was thanks to the prosperous economy, improvements in certain social indicators such as crime, and a general sense of well-being. The country was not involved in war in any part of the world, and unemployment was low. Clinton had also gained some points for his stand against the Republicans in Congress when, in late 1995 and early 1996, they refused to pass a budget and brought the government to a total halt.

Just as Clinton seemed to be heading into his second term from a position of strength, however, a new scandal broke: charges and revelations about financial arrangements during the 1992 campaign by the Democratic National Committee in general, and Clinton and his White House staff in particular. Although most of what was revealed had long been standard conduct of American presidents, Congressmen, and professional political campaigners, Clinton was bruised by some of what was

revealed during the hearings.

Then in 1998 a new scandal surfaced, involving Clinton's sexual conduct with a young female intern. As the facts and charges became public, Clinton equivocated if not outright lied. In February 1999, he became only the second president in American history to be impeached and tried before the Senate. None of the charges got the necessary votes for guilty, but the whole episode left Clinton's image and presidency tarnished.

When he left office, Bill Clinton could point to several achievements: maintaining conditions for unparalleled economic growth and elimination of budget deficits; establishing the North American Free Trade Agreement (NAFTA); the FamilyLeave Act; environmental legislation and executive decisions; the Brady Bill (ban on weapons). But many of his announced goals—health care reform, curtailing campaign spending,improving standards of education—were never pursued with total commitment.If Clinton's presidency had to be characterized by one word, it might be 'frustrating.'

Yet as the first president born after the end of World War II, Clinton did bring something new to the American presidency. He was one of the so-called 'baby-boomers' of the post-war era and he shared many of their tastes and values. He was also a man of the 'new South,' at ease with African-Americans, whether in high office or in gospel churches. He appointed women to high offices. He was the first president to make the nation aware of Asian-Americans as a political force. However historians would rate his accomplishments as a president, Bill Clinton was the representative leader as the nation entered the twenty-first century.

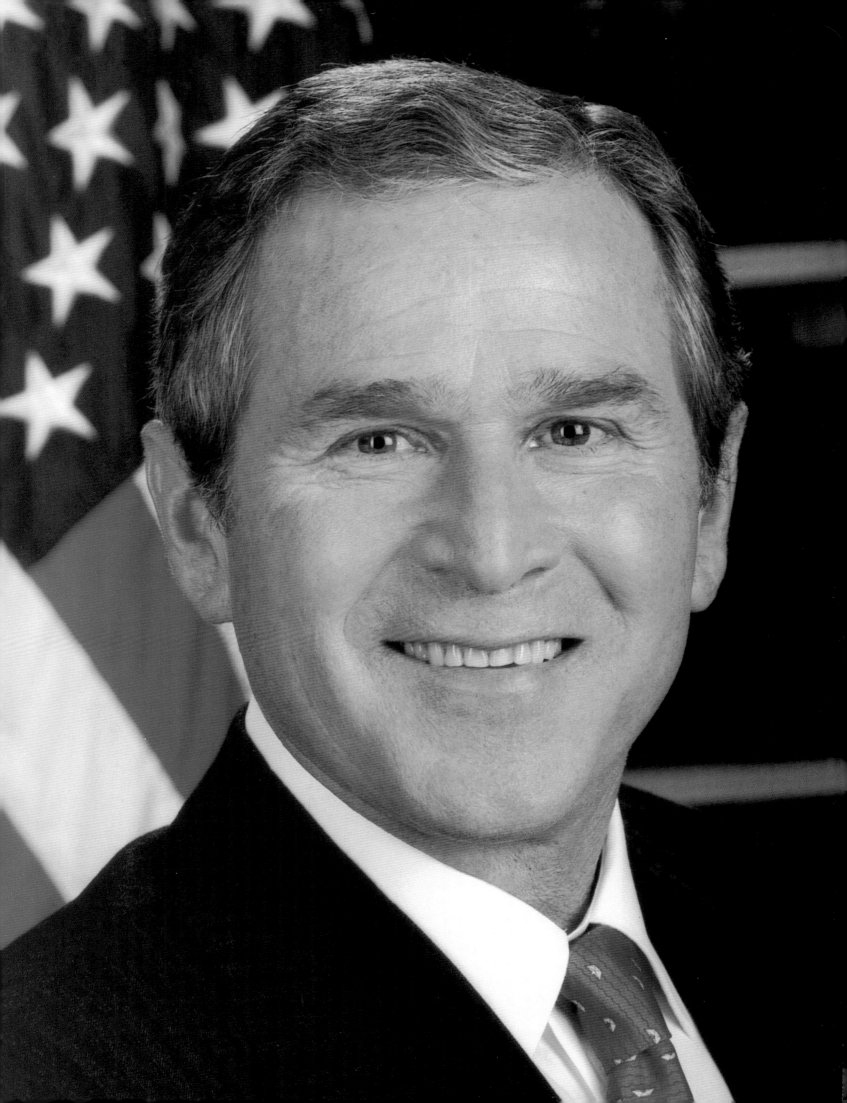

George Walker
BUSH
1946–

When George Walker Bush was inaugurated on 20 January 2001, it marked only the second time in American history that a son of a former president achieved such an honor. But it also brought an end to one of the most tumultuous and controversial episodes in the history of America's presidential campaigns—the disputed Florida vote count.

George W Bush was born in New Haven, Connecticut, but was raised from the age of two in Texas, where his father had moved to enter the oil business. George Herbert Walker Bush would go on to become the 41st president of the United States and this might seem to have enhanced the son's credentials when he ran for the office, but there were some who felt that his path through life had been made all too easy by his father's connections and achievements. He had been 'sent East' to attend the prestigious schools of his father—first Phillips Andover preparatory school, then Yale University, and at both was more noted for his social than academic skills. He returned to work in Texas in the oil business for several years, and in 1973 enrolled in Harvard's highly competitive Business School.

Back in Texas in 1975, Bush was involved in various lucrative deals in oil and gas companies. In 1978, he made his first bid for public office, running for the US House of Representatives. He lost, so he stayed with the oil business. He accepted an offer to join the owners of the Texas Rangers baseball team, and within 9 years would sell his share at a handsome profit. After his father's two terms as Reagan's vice-president, Bush worked closely on both of his father's presidential election campaigns, in 1988 and 1992. With his father's defeat in 1992, Bush became more serious about a career in politics.He ran for governor of Texas in 1994 and narrowly won, but he was easily re-elected in 1998. Although the governor of Texas has limited powers, Bush showed a talent for working with the Democratic opposition and was able to get though legislation on education, juvenile crime, welfare reform, and tort law reform.

Left: *George Walker Bush won the bitterly contested election of 2000 to take office in January 2001.*

Below: *President George W Bush meets with members of Congress in the Oval Office to discuss Medicare reform six weeks after his inauguration.*

Above: *The President and First Lady Laura Bush leave for a weekend at Camp David on 2 March 2001.*

Thanks in part to his father's network of political allies, but also in part to the Republicans' need for an attractive candidate, by 1999 Bush was being promoted as the leading Republican candidate for president in 2000. Backed by the largest 'war chest' in the history of presidential politics, he soon disposed of his only serious challenger in the 2000 primaries, Arizona Senator John McCain, and received his party's nomination in July. His opponent, then Vice-President Albert Gore, seemed to have everything going for him that Bush lacked: decades of service in the federal government, a knowledge and mastery of the details of public issues, and allegedly an ability to articulate and debate that would leave Bush tongue-tied. Yet in the three debates that were carried live on national TV, Bush was able to deal with the issues quite respectably, and from that point on, running on his slogan of 'compassionate conservatism' and a promise to cut back on taxes and the role of the federal government, he ran such a solid campaign that few were willing to predict a winner for the election on 7 November.

In the event, the race was far closer than anyone could ever have imagined. As one by one the states' returns came in on election night, it appeared at first that Gore was going to win, especially when the networks 'awarded' Florida to Gore. When the next day dawned, it turned out that Gore was ahead in the popular vote

and had a lead in the electoral college but that everything would hinge on Florida's still-uncounted votes. At that point, Americans began to get a tutorial in something that only a few students ever really pretended to understand—the electoral college.

Under the procedures stipulated in the US Constitution, American presidents are not elected by a simple majority or plurality of the popular votes. Rather, they are elected by members of the so-called electoral college; these are individuals from each state who are chosen by their respective political parties; their number is determined by the total of national representatives and senators from that state. Each state's popular vote is tallied, and the candidate obtaining the most votes is awarded *all* the votes of the electoral college (although a few states do split the electoral college votes proportionately). This means that, since all of each state's (with those exceptions) electoral college votes go to a candidate even if he leads by only one popular vote, it is possible to win the presidency in the electoral college even when losing the popular vote.

Although most Americans had been taught about this system in their schooldays, many had conveniently forgotten this because the last time it had happened was in 1888, when Grover Cleveland actually got more popular votes than Benjamin Harrison, but Harrison won in the electoral college. By the morning of 8 November 2000, it was clear that the electoral college vote was going to be crucial: if Bush won Florida by one vote, he would get all of Florida's 25 electoral college votes and win; if Gore led by one vote, he would win.

At this point, a new issue beclouded the election. The polls had not even closed when some people in Florida were complaining of voting irregularities—ballots with confusing formats, voting techniques that left intentions unclear, voters denied access, voters unfairly told they were not registered. Some demanded that ballots that had been rejected now be counted, and as the counting proceeded, Americans learned a new word—'chad,' the tiny fragment that hangs from a punctured hole in paper. Meanwhile, the several thousand ballots from Floridians who lived overseas also became crucial, and when it was found that some of these ballots were not in perfect compliance with the regulations, there was a dispute over whether these should be counted.

The upshot of all this was a series of legal contests that mesmerized the nation for several weeks, as lawyers for both candidates went before courts in Florida to argue their positions. In general, Gore's lawyers and supporters argued for extending deadlines and pursuing recounts. But Bush had a slim majority of Florida's popular vote and so his lawyers and supporters argued for holding to tight deadlines and stopping recounts. Eventually the dispute was brought before the US Supreme Court. On 4 December the Justices sent the matter back to the Florida state court for clarification. Then, on 12 December, the Justices decided by a 5-4 vote that it was too late to conduct a recount; in so doing, the court effectively awarded Florida's electoral college votes to Bush. Gore conceded on 13 December.

It was against this background that George W Bush assumed the presidency in January 2001. And it says something—a great deal—about the American people's respect for the rule of law and the office of president that from the moment Bush took the oath of office, the debate over his legitimacy effectively stopped. To be sure, there would be ongoing discussion in the media about the way the election had been decided. And there would eventually be recounts of the Florida votes that could be interpreted to prove whatever the proponents of each side wanted to prove. But by and large, the American people pulled back from the contest that had consumed them during the five weeks following the election and they chose to let George W Bush be their president.

He stirred up some controversy with several of his cabinet nominees, but in the end he got the cabinet he wanted. Bush hit the ground running, seizing the initiative by such actions as proposing federal funds for faith-based social service programs. This particular proposal, which had been one of his campaign promises, eventually lost steam, but it showed that whatever his critics might say about Bush, he was not afraid to stick by the agenda he had campaigned on. Similarly, Bush drew criticism from many when he refused to endorse the Kyoto Treaty on environmental pollution, then decided to withdraw from an antiballistic missile treaty with Russia so that he could proceed to authorize the installation of an elaborate missile defense system.

Through the first months of his presidency, Bush was the butt of more than a few commentators' and comedians' wisecracks about his fracturing of the English language and his casual behavior toward the demands of his job. His supporters, however, portrayed him as a plain-spoken, no-frills, down-to-earth man. As he pushed ahead with his agenda during the first months, Bush won some, lost some—as do all presidents. He did get most of his promised tax cut, though, and although his plan for school vouchers was greatly modified, he did get a major education reform bill through Congress.

All such issues came to a screeching halt on the morning of 11 September 2001, when four hijacked airplanes brought international terrorism led by Al-Qaeda crashing into America's—and the world's—consciousness. Bush rose to the occasion, making hard decisions and blunt statements—referring to the terrorists as 'evildoers,' calling for taking Osama bin Laden 'dead or alive.' Within less than four weeks, he had American planes and missiles raining down on the Taliban and Al-Qaeda in Afghanistan. Soon American troops were on the ground,

Above: *President Bush addresses a joint session of Congress flanked by Vice-President Dick Cheney (l) and House Speaker Dennis Hastert.*

Osama was on the run, the Taliban was defeated, and Afghanistan was freed from the shackles of its militant-fundamentalist regime.

In the wake of 9/11 and Afghanistan, Bush's presidency seemed to be co-opted by the war on terrorism. At home he created a new Department of Homeland Security; offshore he supported the indeterminate and controversial detention of hundreds of potential terrorists at the Guantánamo base along the coast of Cuba. But with victory in Afghanistan assured, Bush began to warn of a new threat: weapons of mass destruction allegedly being developed by Iraq. Rejecting the findings of the UN-sponsored inspectors, he insisted that Iraq posed an immediate threat to the world, and in March 2003 he invaded Iraq with what he would call 'coalition forces,' some 80 percent of which were US troops, with only the British supplying any significant number. After a swift strike from the south, US forces claimed victory in

defend his policies in Iraq, and in campaigning for a second term in the fall of 2004 against the Democratic candidate, John F. Kerry, he refused to weaken his stance. The American public, even while growing increasingly uncomfortable with events in Iraq, were willing to trust Bush to lead the country, and returned him to office.

In his inaugural address in January 2005, Bush stressed his commitment to advancing freedom throughout the world. And when some 60 percent of the eligible Iraqi voters turned out to elect their first government in almost 50 years, Bush was able to claim that the months of struggle in Iraq were beginning to bear fruit. Yet the insurgency promised continuing trouble—and casualties: By spring 2005, the United States alone counted over 1,500 dead and more than 12,000 wounded—many seriously maimed for life.

By the time he was delivering his State of the Union speech in February 2005, Bush was proceeding as though the situation in Iraq was under control and heading into the final phase of US involvement, so he turned his attention to his domestic agenda. In particular, he stressed his intentions to reform Social Security. He was also promising to reform Medicare; he indicated support for an amendment outlawing same-sex marriages; as for the issue of ending abortion rights, it appeared that he would face that if and when it came time to name new Supreme Court justices. He also promised to work to restore good relations with European powers that so strongly opposed the war in Iraq.

Baghdad, and by May Bush was proclaiming an end to the war.

But this did not end the conflict—or casualties—in Iraq. After a period of chaos and confusion, an insurgency developed, made up primarily of disaffected former supporters of Saddam and increasing numbers of Islamic terrorists. Using suicide car bombings, mortar attacks, and explosive devices planted in the road, the insurgents showed no compunction about killing their fellow Iraqis as well as US military. Bush continued to

As he moved into his second term, then, George W Bush continued to show a commitment and consistency that even most of his critics had to concede were the mark of a strong leader. The man who had started as a seemingly passive and conservative president was turning out to be one of the boldest and most innovative.

Above: *President Bush at Ground Zero at the World Trade Center for a memorial service in New York, 11 November 2001. That day the president addressed the General Assembly of the United Nations, stressing the importance to the entire world of the success of the military mission of the United States in Afghanistan.*

Left: *President Bush visited the US troops in Baghdad to celebrate Thanksgiving on 27 November 2003.*

Picture Credits

Adams National Historic Site: page
  19(bottom)
AP Photo/Anja Niedringhaus: page
  198(bottom)
Brompton Picture Library: pages
  19(top), 20(bottom), 21,
  32(center), 34, 36(top), 48, 49,
  51(bottom), 53, 65, 72–3, 82–3,
  110, 112(top), 117, 118(bottom),
  127, 136(all 3), 158(both), 160,
  164(both), 168(top), 174,
  176(top), 182, 185.
Black Star: pages 164–5,
  168(bottom), 169, 172, 173.
Anne S K Brown Library: page 8.
Cincinnati Art Museum: page 47.
DAR Museum: pages 30, 61.
Dwight D. Eisenhower Library:
  pages 148(bottom), 152.
Gerald R Ford Library: pages 175,
  176(bottom).
Harvard College Library
  (Theodore Roosevelt
  Collection): page 105.
Herbert Hoover Presidential
  Library: page 125.
Lyndon B Johnson Library: page
  161.
John F Kennedy Library: pages
  154, 155, 156(both).

Library of Congress: pages 18,
  24(top right and bottom), 25, 40,
  43(top), 44(top), 50, 52, 54,
  60(top), 62, 66, 67(top), 68–9,
  70(bottom), 79, 80, 81, 87,
  89(top), 94–5, 97, 102,
  106(bottom), 107(top), 108–09,
  111(bottom), 113, 114, 115,
  116–17, 119(both), 123(both),
  124, 130(top), 133 (top 2),
  167(bottom).
Monticello: pages 24(left), 29(top).
National Park Service, Washington,
  DC: pages 6(both), 7.
National Portrait Gallery,
  Washington, DC: pages 56–7,
  100.
Peter Newark's Western
  Americana: pages 1, 9(both),
  10–11, 12(both), 13(both),
  14–15, 16, 17(both), 20(top), 22,
  23, 26–7, 28(both), 28–9,
  31(both), 32(top), 33(bottom),
  35(both), 36(bottom), 38, 39, 41,
  42(both), 44(bottom), 45, 55,
  63(both), 64(both), 67(bottom),
  70(top), 71, 75(both), 77, 78, 84,
  85(both), 86, 88, 89(bottom), 90,
  92, 93, 96(both), 98, 101(both),
  103, 104, 106(top), 107(bottom),
  112(bottom), 118(top), 120(top),
  122, 128(both), 129,
  130(bottom), 131, 132(bottom),
  133 (bottom), 134(both),
  135(both), 137, 138, 142, 142–3,
  163(bottom), 166, 170(bottom).
New York Public Library: pages 46,
  51(top), 59, 76, 91(both), 99.
Reuters/Archive Photos: 189, 190,
  191, 192(both), 193.
Reuters/Time Pix/Doug Mills:
  page 197(top).
Reuters/Time Pix/Larry
  Downing: page 198(top).
Reuters/Time Pix/Win McNamee:
  pages 195, 196.
Franklin D Roosevelt Library:
  pages 127, 132(top).
Tennessee State Library: page
  42–43.
TPS/AP: page 184(top).
TPS/Central Press: page 163(top).
TPS/Fox: page 167(top).
TPS/Keystone: pages 141(both),
  146(inset), 149, 150(top),
  152–53(bottom), 157, 159, 162,
  171(both), 177(both),
  180(bottom), 183(top),
  184(bottom).
Truman Library: pages 139, 140.
UPI/Bettmann Newsphotos: pages
  186, 187, 188(both).
US Army: pages 48(top),
  150(bottom), 150–51,
  152–53(bottom).
USIS: page 121.
US National Archives: pages
  33(top), 37, 58, 74(both),
  120(bottom), 146–47, 172–73.
US Naval Historical Center: page
  111(top).
US Navy: page 144.
White House: pages 2, 170(top),
  178, 179, 180(top), 181,
  183(bottom), 184(top).
White House/Eric Draper: page
  194.